United Nations
Medals and Ribbons
for Peacekeeping

by

Colonel Frank Foster

Library of Congress Catalog Card Number -2020934596
Hardcover Edition ISBN -978-1-884452-76-5
Softcover Edition ISBN - 978-1-884452-77-2
Copyright 2020 by MOA PRESS

Published by:

MOA Press (Medals of America Press)
114 Southchase Blvd
Fountain Inn, SC 29644-9137
www.moapress.com
Version 2020.07.22

COLONEL
FRANK FOSTER

COL. FRANK C. FOSTER *(Ret.)*, obtained his BS from The Citadel, MBA from the University of Georgia and is a graduate of the Army's Command and General Staff College and War College. He saw service as a Battery Commander in Germany and served in Vietnam with the 173rd Airborne Brigade and USARV General Staff. In the Adjutant General's Corps, he served as the Adjutant General of the Central Army Group, the 4th Infantry Division and was the Commandant and Chief of the Army's Adjutant General's Corps from 1986 to 1990. His military service provided him a unique understanding of the Armed Forces Awards System. He currently operates Medals of America Press and is the author of the *Military Medals of America*, numerous books on the Air Force, Marines and Navy awards and author of *Medals and Insignia of the Republic of Vietnam*. He and his wife Linda, who was decorated with the Army Commander's Medal in 1990 for service to the Army, live in Greenville, South Carolina.

Grateful Acknowledgements

The author wishes to express his deepest appreciation to the following individuals for their invaluable contributions. Without their unselfish efforts, this book would have ended as an unfilled dream.

The entire Medals of America team with special thanks to:

Mrs. Linda Brailsford Foster for the splendid job in editing this book (several times over).

Mr. Augusto Meneses, Design Director of ADDMedia Creatives for his most excellent work in preparing this book.

Mr. Kirk Stotzer, Art Director and Ms. "Buz" Buswell - Pre Press.

The late **Lonny Borts** for work in developing this book.

Col. (Ret.) Charles Mugno, Director of the Institute of Heraldry.

Lt. Col. Ugo Pastorino and **Mr. Kris Stasiewicz** of the *United Nations Field Administration and Logistics Division* for their invaluable assistance in gathering data on the UN medals, ribbons and clasps and their applications to the appropriate peace-keeping operations.

Mr. Fred Schottler, Information Officer of the *United Nations Peace & Security Programs Section* for supplying a wealth of vital data and descriptions of past and ongoing UN peace-keeping missions.

Mr. John Sylvester, for other Peacekeeping awards.

Mr. Steve Himes and **Mrs. Terri Himes** for their technical assistance in getting the book on different production platforms.

Introduction

Twenty five years ago I was going through all of my military awards reference books and noticed after a while that there was not one anywhere on the United Nations medals. A call to the late Lonny Borts (Dean of American Military Ribbons) led to a quick agreement. He would research and write on United Nations medals and Ribbons and I would edit, illustrate and publish it.

That was 1997 and the book proved popular and a steady seller. Eventually the entire print run sold out and in my head the subject had been covered so time to move on. Then several years ago I started updating other military awards books which had sold out and finally came back to the UN book. WOW! was it ever out of date. Unfortunately Lonny had passed away so "OK", I'll just update it and do a new edition...Wrong answer. The deeper I got into updating the medals (and they are not that easy to fine sometimes) the more I begin to appreciate the determination of the UN in carrying out its peacekeeping missions often in the most difficult and sometimes fatal circumstance.

The final results is an all new book with almost twice as many medals as before and the opportunity to do it in all color. It has been a road of despair at times as you follow the trials of misery in the world of peacekeeping but also exhilarating savoring the success of the good guys in blue helmets.

In the more than seventy years of its existence, UN Peacekeeping has evolved significantly as an important tool of international crisis response and has proven to be an essential instrument for global peace and security over many years. Today fourteen peacekeeping operations around the world illustrate the wide range of strategies and resources the United Nations brings together from its member countries in support of peace and security. Now in the 21st Century, UN peacekeeping missions are called upon to deploy to increasingly difficult and complex environments, with the demand for a total peacekeeping package that can include all the aspects of Nation building.

Peacekeeping is one of the most effective tools available to the United Nations in the promotion and maintenance of international peace and security. Yet the actual peacekeepers are challenged where political solutions are often absent, and their mission may seem to lack focus and clear priorities. Violent environments have caused a rise in fatalities and injuries of peacekeepers and missions often struggle with the lack of the right personnel and equipment to meet these threats. And yet the military, police and civilian peacekeepers from hundreds of countries continue to respond when called upon for their service.

How to reward and honor the service of the Peacekeepers? As with most questions the answer leads to Rome. It was the Roman Legions who first organized an awards system for honoring their soldiers for bravery and service. Once recognized, Roman soldiers wore these decorations in battle, parades and displayed them in their homes after military service.

Two thousand years later almost every nation and country uses medals to reward and honor the service of their soldiers. So it is in this tradition that the UN has established a system of "campaign" or "mission " medals to acknowledge and reward the troops, police and civilian personnel who carry out the boots on the ground part of every peacekeeping mission. This practice was continued for all subsequent operations and today there are almost 70 such awards for service with the United Nations.

UN Peacekeeping Service Medals are special in that the medallion is always the same but the medal drape and ribbon are unique in the use of heraldic colors to clearly identify the mission. Until this book I do not know of another single source that tells the meaning of each ribbon.

So the practice of authorizing service medals to commemorate each operation was conceived and appropriate awards designed, struck and bestowed upon participating military personnel. Although the UN contains many specialized agencies dealing with such diverse subjects as aviation, health, communications, etc., it is the basic premise of this book to deal only with the peace-keeping operations and the medals, ribbons and clasps that arose from each mission. Since the basic motivation is to illustrate the medals and their mission and not political, we endeavor to present a picture of the background, activities and effects of each mission but limit the descriptions to basic facts and leave the endless interpretations to the historians.

I trust that this approach will meet favor with the reader/enthusiast and the book will be approached in terms of its informational value on the peacekeeping medals rather than as an in-depth study of the United Nations peace keeping operations.

And then there is that ugly word "mistakes". As hard as we try, we know there will be mistakes in this book. Therefore please send all comments, suggestions and corrections in care of the publisher. Thank you for using this book. In so doing, you honor the service of all our United Nations Peacekeepers.

Frank Foster

Table of Contents

The idea of uniting the countries of the earth in an organization to maintain peace is not a new concept. However, it wasn't until the early 20th century that the first serious attempt to put the idea into practice, the League of Nations, arose from the carnage of the First World War.

As originally conceived by its founder, U.S. President Woodrow Wilson, the member nations of the League would pledge to preserve the independence and territory of its members against attack and agree to submit all disputes to arbitration or investigation. If agreements could not be reached, the member nations could apply economic sanctions or, as a last resort, use military force against an aggressor nation. These are not unlike the principles behind the formation of the United Nations some 25 years later, but with some serious differences.

League of Nations at its opening session Geneva, November 1920. UN Photo

Unfortunately, the statesmen who proposed the League of Nations were not prepared for the outpouring of nationalism, suspicion and reinterpretation of principles that accompanied the rhetoric and high moral beliefs espoused by its founders. France, for example, believed that the League was formed only to monitor and prevent the emergence of a rearmed Germany. Soviet Russia viewed the alliance as an imperialist plot to avert the rise of Communism. Great Britain seemed willing to fully debate all issues but without being forced to take definitive action and, finally, Japan and Italy, two of its founding nations, disregarded the entire concept of world peace by engaging in policies of blatant imperialism and expansionism.

The chances for success were also seriously diminished when President Wilson could not convince the U.S. Senate to approve the treaty under which the United States would have become a member nation. In a classic example of the isolationist attitude that would prevail until the advent of World War II, the Senate feared that membership would burden the United States with involuntary obligations in areas where there was no real U.S. national interest.

The League did manage to bring a few small conflicts between nations to an end, (e.g.: Greece & Bulgaria in 1925 and Poland & Lithuania in 1927) but the major struggles involving powerful nations such as Japan's conquest of Manchuria in 1933, Italy's attack on Ethiopia in 1935 and the Soviet Union's winter war against Finland in 1939 brought nothing stronger than condemnation or expulsion from the League.

The advent of World War II led to the ultimate demise of the League of Nations but did not dampen the fervent desire by the nations of the free world to revive the concept of a meaningful world peace-keeping body which would not repeat the mistakes of the past.

The first inkling that such a new world body might be in the making was the Inter-Allied Declaration signed in London in 1941 by the U.S., Great Britain, the Commonwealth Nations and nine governments-in-exile declaring the need for a cooperative organization to keep the world free from aggression.

In 1942, representatives of the major Allied nations met in Washington, DC to sign a brief document known as the Declaration by the United Nations, which affirmed the principles of the Atlantic Charter signed the previous year and marked the first time the term, "United Nations" had ever been officially used.

The United Nations Charter was formulated at the San Francisco Conference held in 1945. Later that year, the United Nations, as we know it today, came into being with its ratification by the first 51 member nations.

First Session of the Security Council at Church House, London 1946. UN Photo

In the years that have elapsed since that ratification, the United Nations has dealt with everything from minor disputes and controversies to bloody skirmishes and localized wars and, without doubt, it has played a major role in keeping the powder keg of the atomic era from erupting. United Nations Peacekeeping began in 1948 when the Security Council authorized the deployment of UN military observers to the Middle East. The mission's role was to monitor the Armistice Agreement between Israel and its Arab neighbours – an operation which became known as the United Nations Truce Supervision Organization (UNTSO).

Since then, more than 70 peacekeeping operations have been deployed by the UN. Over the years, hundreds of thousands of military personnel, as well as tens of thousands of UN police and other civilians from more than 120 countries have participated in UN peacekeeping operations.

Unfortunately the cost has been high not only in treasure and materiels but more than 3,000 UN peacekeepers from some 120 countries have died while serving under the UN flag.

The Early Years (1948-1988)

UN Peacekeeping was born at a time when Cold War rivalries frequently paralyzed the Security Council and peacekeeping was primarily limited to maintaining cease fires and stabilizing political situations on the ground as well as providing crucial support for political efforts to resolve conflict by peaceful means.

Early missions generally consisted of unarmed military observers or lightly armed troops with the primary role of monitoring, reporting and confidence-building. The first two peacekeeping operations deployed by the UN were the UN Truce Supervision Organization (UNTSO) and the UN Military Observer Group in India and Pakistan (UNMOGIP). These first missions, which continue operating to this day, are examples of the observation and monitoring type of operation and have authorized strengths in the low hundreds of unarmed UN military observers.

In 1950, when the forces of North Korea invaded the Republic of South Korea, the UN Security Council adopted a resolution calling for its member nations to use military force to restore peace. Three years later, after military participation by 16 nations and logistical support from 25 other countries, the UN arranged an armistice. It was the first time in history that a united military action had been successfully initiated and fought under the auspices of a world body against aggression. This pattern was to be followed by many such cooperative actions, albeit on a smaller scale, in the years to come.

The first armed peacekeeping operation in 1956 was the First UN Emergency Force (UNEF I) deployed successfully to defuse the Suez Crisis.

In 1960 the UN Operation in the Congo (ONUC), was the first large-scale mission with nearly 20,000 military personnel at its peak. ONUC demonstrated the risks involved in trying to bring stability to war-torn regions. 250 UN personnel died and many more wounded or injured while serving on that mission, including the death of Secretary-General Dag Hammarskjold.

In the 1960s and 1970s, the UN established short-term missions in the Dominican Republic (unusual in that no medal was issued for DOMREP), West New Guinea (West Irian) ,(UNSF), and Yemen (UNYOM), plus starting long term deployments in Cyprus (UNFICYP) and the Middle East (UNEF II), UN Disengagement Observer Force (UNDOF) and UN Interim Force in Lebanon (UNIFIL). The Nobel Peace Prize was awarded to UN peacekeepers in 1988. With the Nobel Committee stating *"the United Nations Peacekeeping Forces through their efforts have made important contributions towards the realization of one of the fundamental tenets of the United Nations. Thus, the world organization has come to play a more central part in world affairs and has been invested with increasing trust".*

The Post-Cold War (1945-1990)

As the Cold War ended, the overall complexity for UN Peacekeeping changed dramatically from field operations and "traditional" missions generally involving observational tasks by military personnel to complex "multidimensional" missions. These expanded multidimensional missions were needed to ensure comprehensive peace agreements and assist in helping troubled countries lay the foundations for sustainable peace.

The nature of the crisis also changed over the years. UN Peacekeeping, originally developed as a means of dealing with external State conflicts, became increasingly being sent to internal State conflicts and civil wars.

The roles of UN Peacekeepers expanded to a wide variety of complex tasks: helping to build sustainable government institutions, monitoring human rights, reforming military and police organizations, plus the very difficult and expensive task of disarmament, demobilization and reintegration of former combatants.

While the military personnel remained the backbone of most peacekeeping operations, the many new peacekeeping jobs required:

- Administrators and Economists
- Police officers and Legal experts
- Landmine and bomb De-miners
- Electoral observers and Human rights monitors
- Civil affairs and Governance specialists
- Humanitarian and Social workers
- Communications and Public information experts

The Early 90s: Growing Missions

The end of the Cold war saw a new consensus and greater common sense of purpose in the Security Council. Between 1989 and 1994 there was a rapid increase of 20 new peacekeeping operations raising the peacekeepers force from 11,000 to 75,000.

Peacekeeping operations were established in such countries as Angola (UNAVEM I) and (UNAVEM II), Cambodia (UNTAC), El Salvador (ONUSAL), Mozambique (ONUMOZ) and Namibia

(UNTAG), with the mandate to help implement complex peace agreements; stabilize the security; re-organize local military and police and supervising the elections of new democratic governments.

Unfortunately, the general success of earlier missions raised expectations for UN Peacekeeping beyond its ability based on its operational rules of engagement. This came to the painful front in the mid 1990's when the Security Council was not able to authorize sufficiently strong mandates or provide adequate resources for many missions.

Missions where fighting continued, such as the former Yugoslavia (UNPROFOR), Rwanda (UNAMIR) and Somalia (UNOSOM II), created very difficult operations where there was no peace to keep. These high-profile peacekeeping operations came under criticism as UN peacekeepers were faced with warring parties failing to keep peace agreements, or where the peacekeepers themselves were out gunned and not provided sufficient resources or political support. Civilian casualties rose and fighting continued dealing a blow to the reputation of UN Peacekeeping.

These setbacks caused the Security Council to limit new peacekeeping missions and begin a program of reviewing operational problems to prevent such future failures. An independent inquiry looked into United Nations actions during the 1994 genocide in Rwanda and provided the UN General Assembly a comprehensive assessment on the 1993-1995 events in Srebrenica in the former Yugoslavia. The reasons for the UN withdrawal from Somalia were also reviewed and studied .

During the last five years of the 20th Century UN peacekeepers continued long-term operations in the Middle East, Asia and Cyprus. Continuing crises in a number of countries and regions reaffirmed the need for vigorous UN Peacekeeping. The Security Council authorized new UN operations in Angola (UNAVEM III) and (MONUA); Bosnia and Herzegovina (UNMIBH); Croatia (UNCRO), Eastern Slavonia, Baranja and Western Sirmium (UNTAES) and (UNPSG); North Macedonia (UNPREDEP); Guatemala (MINUGUA) and Haiti (UNSMIH),(UNTMIH) and (MIPONUH).

Of more than passing interest at this point, it should noted that during the first 25 years of UN existence, some 11 observer missions or peace-keeping operations were mounted around the world. By comparison, the second 25 years saw the number nearly triple.

UN Photo

Peacekeepings' Postive World Impact

UN Peacekeeping efforts were validated early 2000s when a RAND Corporation study showed the UN peacekeeping as successful in two out of three efforts. It also found UN nation-building efforts in seven out of eight UN cases resulted in peace. A Human Security Report in the same time period documented a decline in the number of wars, genocides and human rights abuses since the end of the Cold War and attributed that international missions led by the UN contributed to the decline in armed conflict since the end of the Cold War.

Lessons Learned 1990-1999

Unfortunately, the UN has also drawn criticism for failures where the Security Council has failed to pass resolutions or the member states have been reluctant to support efforts in the face of deteriorating conditions. Security Council Disagreements are viewed as having failed to prevent the 1994 Rwandan genocide. UN and international inaction has been criticized for failing to intervene and provide sufficient humanitarian aid during the Second Congo War or prevent the 1995 Srebrenica massacre and provide humanitarian aid in Somalia. Other disappointments were the failing to implement provisions of Security Council resolutions on the the Israeli–Palestinian conflict, Kashmir dispute and continuing failure to prevent genocide or provide assistance in Darfur.

To address the problem of delays in actually getting boots on the ground during sudden crisis the UN is working on developing a rapid reaction force. This will be a standing force, administered by the UN and deployed by the Security Council. Troops and support ready for quick deployment in the event of future genocides or emergences would come from current Security Council members.

Another reoccurring problem has been UN peacekeepers being accused of sexual abuse including child rape, gang rape, and soliciting prostitutes during missions in the Congo, Haiti, Liberia, Sudan, Burundi, and Côte d'Ivoire. In response the UN has taken steps toward reforming its operations and providing stronger leadership and standards of conduct. The Brahimi Report was to review former peacekeeping missions, identify problems, and take steps to correct misconduct and ensure the higher standards of future peacekeeping missions. UN operations have worked to learn and improve from past mistakes for future peacekeeping operations. In 2008 a capstone doctrine entitled "United Nations Peacekeeping Operations: Principles and Guidelines" incorporated lessons learned. A 'Peace Operations 2010' reform agenda has been published to apply the enhanced standards. UN Peacekeeping anti-corruption guidance and oversight has also been subject to review and improvement.

In the first 10 years of the 21th Century UN Peacekeeping forces were stretched like never before and increasingly called upon to deploy to remote, uncertain operating environments and into volatile political situations. Peacekeeping missions became more expensive and increasingly complex, requiring viable transition strategies for missions where a degree of stability has been attained, and often turn on a dime to meet uncertain future requirements. By 2010 UN Peacekeeping entered a phase of mission consolidation where for the first time requirements began to slightly decline, seeing reduction of troops in the Democratic Republic of the Congo and the withdrawal of UN Mission in the Central African Republic and Chad at the end of 2010. Today in 2020, there are about 110,000 military, police and civilian staff serving in 14 peacekeeping missions, representing a decrease in both personnel and peacekeeping missions, as a result of increased peaceful transitions and the slow rebuilding of functioning states.

New UN Operations and Challenges

However the challenges faced by the UN are not diminishing. The emergence of new conflicts means the demand for peacekeeping missions will remain high and peacekeeping will continue to be one of the UN's most complex and expensive world wide operational tasks.

Combined with the political complexity facing peacekeeping operations and their mandates, both military and civilian side, remain very broad. Specialized capabilities, police, economic development, education and resettlement will be in especially high demand over the coming years.

In October 2014, the UN Secretary-General established a 17-member High-level Independent Panel on UN Peace Operations to make a comprehensive assessment of the state of UN peace operations and the emerging needs of the future. The HIPPO report, as it is known, was issued in June 2015, with key recommendations for the way forward for peace operations. The UN multidimensional peacekeeping program is set to keep facilitating the political process, protect civilians, assist in the disarmament, demobilization and reintegration of former combatanats; support the organization of elections, protect and promote human rights and assist in restoring the rule of law.

The Peacekeeping Medals that are shown on the following pages are the United Nations postive way of honoring the military, police and support personnel who actually carry out the Mandates of the UN Security Council in its quest for world peace.

How much does peacekeeping cost?

The approved budget for UN Peacekeeping operations for the fiscal year 1 July 2019 - 30 June 2020 is $6.5 billion.

This amount finances 12 of the 13 United Nations peacekeeping missions, supports logistics for the African Union Mission in Somalia (AMISOM), and provides support, technology and logistics to all peace operations through global service centers in Brindisi (Italy) and a regional service centre in Entebbe (Uganda). The remaining two peacekeeping missions, the UN Truce Supervision Organisation (UNTSO) and the UN Military Observer Group in India and Pakistan (UNMOGIP), are financed through the UN regular budget.

By way of comparison, this is less than half of one per cent of world military expenditures (estimated at $1,747 billion in 2013).

The 2019-2020 budget represents an average of 1.9% reduction on the approved budget for 2018-2019. The top 10 providers of assessed contributions to United Nations Peacekeeping operations for 2019 are:

1. United States (27.89%)
2. China (15.21%)
3. Japan (8.56%)
4. Germany (6.09%)
5. United Kingdom (5.79%)
6. France (5.61%)
7. Italy (3.30%)
8. Russian Federation (3.04%)
9. Canada (2.73%)
10. Republic of Korea (2.26%)

If almost 7 billion dollars seems a huge amount in the greater scope of nations and gobal trade it may be the best investment our countries can make. For if there was no UN peacekeeping operations then who? Who would strive to settle disputes between Nations, settle Civil Wars, develop repect for human rights, build democracies and strive to make our world a better place to live?

Truly the United Nations and its Peacekeeping missions are one of the great success stories of our world over the past 70 years. Cheap at twice the price many will say.

UN Photo

History of the United Nations Emblem

A. First Logo Concept

B. Second Logo Concept

C. Protype UN Badge

The United Nations emblem, the universally recognized symbol of the seventy five year old peace organization, came into existence at the same time the UN was created. The insignia, which now adorns every conceivable item of United Nations property from stationery and medals to helmets and ambulances, originated as part of an identification badge worn by attendees to the San Francisco Conference held in 1945. Since the United States was the host country for the Conference, members of the U.S. State Department were given the assignment, never realizing the countless millions of people who would see their work in the years that followed.

The task at hand was to create an elementary but appropriate symbol to express the desire for peace in the post-war world. The various suggestions that were considered by the State Department group in the transition from initial concept to final design are presented on this page and on the following page.

Initial brainstorming sessions produced a number of potential designs that were interesting but not truly suitable. The first of these logo concepts (item a. at left) was the simplest from a graphical standpoint, depicting the letters "UN" in lower case Roman letters. However, while it was long on simplicity, it fell very short on significance. Its main advantage seemed to be the ability to be read upside-down but the designers soon realized that it was meaningless to more than half the world.

The second attempt (item b.) depicted bundles of sheathes wrapped in olive branches to represent togetherness and cooperation amongst the free peoples of the world. However, the result was deemed uncomfortably close to the symbol of Mussolini's Fascist regime and it, too, was discarded.

After these first few attempts, the concept of a map was proposed and was instantly embraced as the ideal method to express the then-popular "One-World" concept advanced by one-time U.S. presidential candidate, Wendell Willkie. Of all the cartographic systems in use, the one which best met the requirements was the polar azimuthal equidistant projection which depicted all land masses in a circle, with the north pole at the exact center.

This map was favored at the time by the military for plotting aircraft bombing and ferry missions and had found its way into civilian life via newspaper reports of the war's progress. Although the sizes of the Earth's territories are distorted at the extreme edges, the group deemed the concept highly workable and the prototype United Nations badge (item c. on the previous page) was then designed.

Further suggestions were made to add a semi-circular leaf pattern under the map to enhance the message of peace. The configuration chosen initially was a display of laurel leaves similar to that which embellished the company logo of the Philco Corporation (item d. to the right), a leading manufacturer of communications equipment. However, recognizing that the laurel leaves are a symbol of victory, not peace, cooler heads prevailed and olive branches, the universal sign of peace and harmony, were substituted in the final logo design (item e.).

In the matter of a suitable base color for the badge, it is quite interesting to note that the same group also created the pigment now recognized world-wide as United Nations blue. Upon some deep reflection, it seemed highly appropriate to select a color that was not present in the flag of any member nation and, to this end, the now-familiar smoky shade of light blue was chosen. In honor of Edward R. Stettinius, U.S. Secretary of State and leader of the United States delegation to the conference, the color was designated "Stettinius Blue".

The delegates' badge (item f.) was then manufactured in smoky light blue jeweler's enamel featuring both the newly-approved UN emblem and the text in bright gold and white. An identical design which substituted a flame red enamel for the light blue was struck to identify accredited members of the press corps that were to cover the conference.

The basic pattern of a light blue field with all details executed in pure white framed in gold, first unveiled at the San Francisco in 1945, remains in its original form on all United Nations paraphernalia to this day.

D. Philco Corporate Logo

E. Final UN Logo Design

F. Conference Delegate's Badge

Current United Nations Symbols

UN Medal Korea French Variation

UNGOMAP

UN Medal Clasp

UN Flag

UN Cap Badge

UN Patch

Service Ribbon

KOREA

Lapel Pin

Hat Pin

UN Medal Current Variation

IN THE SERVICE OF PEACE

FOR SERVICE IN DEFENCE OF THE PRINCIPLES OF THE CHARTER OF THE UNITED NATIONS

UN Medal Korean Variation

Miniature Medal

Blue helmet worn by United Nations peace-keeping personnel.

The primary symbol of this concept is the United Nations Emblem, universally used within the UN on its flag, cap badge and medals, as well as all headquarters buildings, vehicles and field installations. The central motif of a polar projection of the world sheathed in a wreath of olive branches is fully described, along with its history, starting on page 10.

Until recently, individual countries participating in UN peace-keeping operations had the option to design, manufacture and distribute unique organizational insignia, usually in the form of shoulder patches, for wear by their troops in the field. However, with the number of participating nations on the rise and the scope of the missions expanding, the concept of a "uniform" was fast being compromised. Another important consideration was the matter of security as troops had difficulty recognizing the distinguishing marks of other UN contingents. For these reasons, all these attempts at individuality are no longer authorized for wear. In their place, the shoulder patch depicted in the right-center of the page to the left is the only "soft" insignia article used on the uniform, both as a shoulder patch and as part of the Military Police sleeve brassard.

Since its inception, the United Nations has striven to maintain the highest possible level of physical visibility for personnel attached to its operations and missions in the field. As originally conceived, bright colors on flags, uniform items and accessories were to be a means of providing a measure of security for troops whose primary task was peace-keeping in those areas where hostile actions were commonplace. Phrased another way, the idea was to "tell the good guys from the bad guys."

The illustrations on the page to the left depict the use of the United Nations emblem on the flag and items of uniform apparel and medals.

World Approach to UN Operations & Awards

UN Photo

The emergence of the United Nations as a major factor on the international scene undoubtedly presented a problem for military commanders forced to operate under sets of rules not of their own making. However, the awards policies of the nations contributing forces to the various UN missions remain, to this day, strictly a function of local prerogative.

Initially, the countries involved carried on an awards policy of "business as usual". Although the UN issued the United Nations Korean Medal to commemorate the Korean action, most of the countries who contributed troops to that "police action" issued their own individual awards. Samples of 12 such awards are presented as item 1 on the facing page (only the ribbons are shown for conciseness). It is to be noted that the British ribbon (b.) was used by most of the Commonwealth Nations (e.g.: Canada, Australia and New Zealand) but South Africa created its own (k.). The Canadian Voluntary Service Medal for Korea (c.) is a relatively new award. An unusual case was Denmark which issued one medal for those who served on the hospital ship, Jutland (item f.) and another for medical personnel who participated in the exchange of prisoners-of-war in 1953 (item g.).

Other United Nations members created similar commemorative awards but many chose to simply accept the United Nations Service Medal and issue no distinctive medal of their own.

With the establishment of the United Nations Medal, the policy towards creation of individual medals for the various UN missions seemed to take a dramatic turn. This is probably due to the nature of the newer peace-keeping operations which were much smaller in scope than Korea with few actual battles being fought by the mission participants. Another factor may have been the reluctance to repeat the Korean experience wherein most participants received TWO awards for the same action. Whatever the motivation, since that time, with only a few isolated exceptions (Ghana, Ireland and The Netherlands just to name a few) the United Nations Medal and the unique ribbons that commemorate each mission have been considered sufficient to reward the individual participants in a UN mission.

Another major difference is the manufacturing of United Nations ribbon to comply with the regulations of individual countries. To illustrate this, item 2 on the next page shows various United Nations ribbons as manufactured to local width and finish requirements in the United States, Great Britain, the Netherlands and Thailand.

Once the hurdle of medal issuance was overcome, the United Nations then had to deal with the individual manner in which their awards were worn on the uniforms of affiliate nations. Classic among the policies and attitudes prevailing towards UN awards is the United States. For over 40 years (exclusive of Korea), any U.S. personnel who participated in a UN activity were permitted to wear the United Nations Medal but NOT the distinctive ribbon of the specific mission. The only ribbon acceptable on the U.S. military uniform was the UNTSO ribbon. The author was recently asked to research the origin of this strange policy but could find no directive, order, edict or decree which set forth the practice, nor was there anyone in the various military departments or the Department of Defense whose memory dated back to its origins.

It therefore came as no surprise when, under pressure from the UN, the DOD announced that the policy on the wear of United Nations awards was to be changed but, typically, in a very singular fashion. Acceptance of all UN ribbons was approved but only the FIRST ribbon and/or medal awarded may actually be worn. All subsequent UN operations are denoted by the placement of a small (3/16" dia.) bronze star on the suspension ribbon of the medal and on the ribbon bar, one for each new mission. Subsequent tours of duty with the SAME peace-keeping mission, presently denoted by silver numerals (item 7, page 34), are not recognized. The French government maintains the same policy for any United Nations awards.

Contrast this policy with that of Canada and Great Britain which allow all United Nations medals to be worn with appropriate devices and clasps. Examples of these three different systems are shown as items 1, 2 and 3 on page 18. Item 1 is a ribbon display of a U.S. Serviceman who has participated in a number of recent UN operations. Item 2 depicts a group of Canadian ribbons worn in conjunction with UN awards and item 3 is a similar array of British awards.

The order of precedence prescribed by the three nations is as interesting as it is diverse. Canada groups all UN ribbons together directly after decorations and their own service awards but before commemorative and long service ribbons. Great Britain, on the other hand, mixes UN awards with their own service awards ("war medals") and displays them in chronological order of acceptance. Finally, the precedence established by the United States, locates the UN medals after all decorations, unit, good conduct and service awards. Lastly, item 3 on on the facing page presents a sample display of miniature UN medals as worn on evening dress uniforms by military personnel and on formal civilian attire.

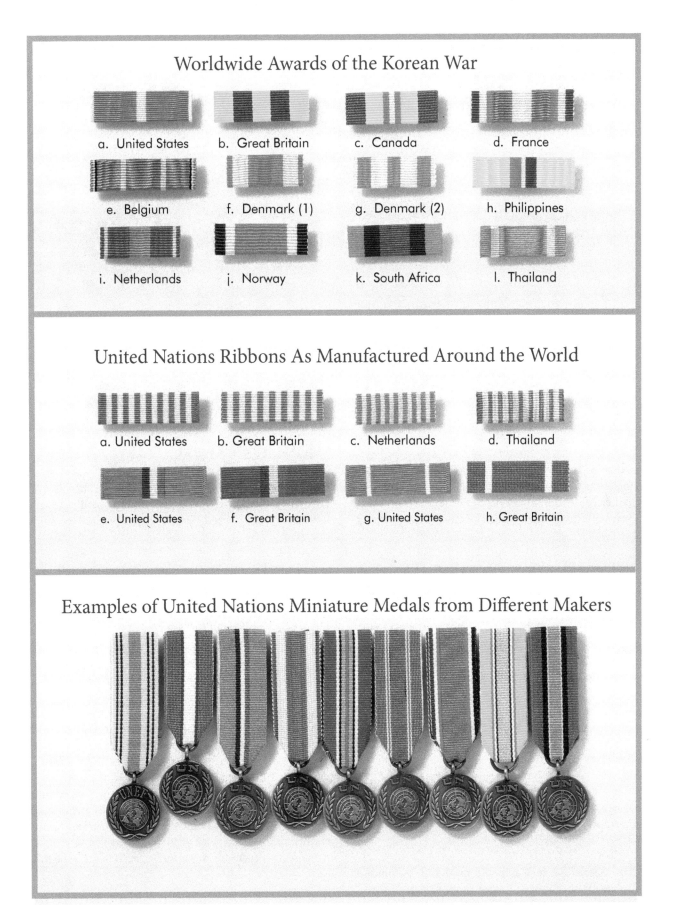

Worldwide Awards of the Korean War

a. United States
b. Great Britain
c. Canada
d. France

e. Belgium
f. Denmark (1)
g. Denmark (2)
h. Philippines

i. Netherlands
j. Norway
k. South Africa
l. Thailand

United Nations Ribbons As Manufactured Around the World

a. United States
b. Great Britain
c. Netherlands
d. Thailand

e. United States
f. Great Britain
g. United States
h. Great Britain

Examples of United Nations Miniature Medals from Different Makers

United Nations Clasps & Devices

1. CONGO Clasp

2. UNGOMAP Clasp

3. OSGAP Clasp

4. UNAMIC Clasp

5. UNSMIH Clasp

6. Proposed UNSSM Clasps

7. Silver Numeral Devices

As in other medallic systems throughout the world, the United Nations employs a series of medal clasps and ribbon devices to denote additional service in a specific theater of operations or to indicate when a medal has been awarded for efforts beyond its original scope.

This was the case when UN troops sent to the Congo (ONUC) were awarded the UNTSO medal/ribbon along with a clasp containing the name, CONGO (item 1 above). However, a distinctive ribbon was later designed and the clasp was discontinued.

Another such instance is the Afghanistan/Pakistan mission, UNGOMAP, for which no specific medal was established. To commemorate the operation a clasp, UNGOMAP (item 2) was issued to personnel who were drawn from three other UN operations. The larger clasp was worn on the medal and the smaller on the ribbon bar of the parent organization, UNTSO, UNDOF or UNIFIL.

Another clasp (item 3) was created to commemorate the successor activity to UNGOMAP known as the Office of the Secretary-General for Afghanistan/Pakistan (OSGAP). This clasp (only one size this time) is apparently unofficial and is only worn by assigned Canadian personnel, again on the "parent" medal/ribbon (UNTSO, UNDOF or UNIFIL).

The UN operations in Cambodia produced an unusual medal/clasp situation. Since the advance mission (UNAMIC) was quite short in duration, a clasp (item 4) was designed and manufactured for wear on the medal of the successor mission (UNTAC). Before it could be distributed to qualifying personnel, however, the clasp was discontinued and a distinctive ribbon was designed.

A later UN mission, the United Nations Support Mission in Haiti (UNSMIH), is a direct follow-on to the UNMIH operation and uses the same medal/ribbon as UNMIH with a clasp, UNSMIH. Item 5 is an artist's conception of the new item.

The United Nations Special Service Medal will be issued with clasps to identify the region where the medal was earned. No clasps have been approved as of this writing but, when authorized, they will bear the name of the appropriate country or United Nations organization. Item 6 above is an artist's conception of two proposed clasps for overseas service with UN offices that are not connected with a specific peace-keeping operation.

Since 1974, Arabic numerals in metallic silver (item 7) are awarded to personnel who have served more than one tour of duty with a specific peace-keeping mission. The numeral is affixed to the medal and service ribbon to indicate the total number of tours of duty. The ribbon itself represents the initial assignment, the numeral 2 indicates the second tour, the numeral 3 the third tour, etc.

United Nations Ribbons Examples

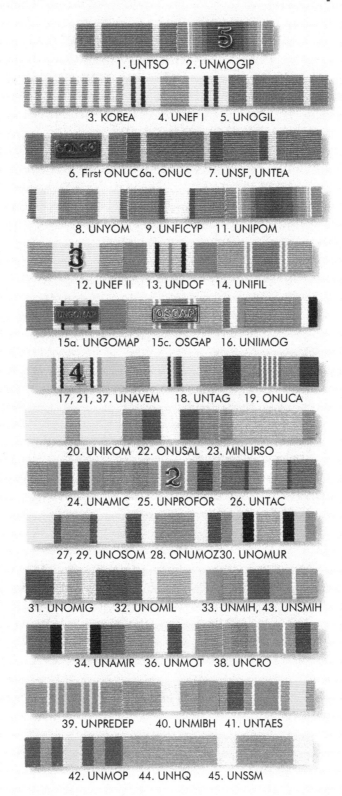

1. UNTSO   2. UNMOGIP

3. KOREA   4. UNEF I   5. UNOGIL

6. First ONUC 6a. ONUC   7. UNSF, UNTEA

8. UNYOM   9. UNFICYP   11. UNIPOM

12. UNEF II   13. UNDOF   14. UNIFIL

15a. UNGOMAP   15c. OSGAP   16. UNIIMOG

17, 21, 37. UNAVEM   18. UNTAG   19. ONUCA

20. UNIKOM   22. ONUSAL   23. MINURSO

24. UNAMIC   25. UNPROFOR   26. UNTAC

27, 29. UNOSOM   28. ONUMOZ 30. UNOMUR

31. UNOMIG   32. UNOMIL   33. UNMIH, 43. UNSMIH

34. UNAMIR   36. UNMOT   38. UNCRO

39. UNPREDEP   40. UNMIBH   41. UNTAES

42. UNMOP   44. UNHQ   45. UNSSM

NOTE: *This ribbon chart illustrates all of the service awards of the United Nations arranged in approximate chronological order for the first 50 years of peace-keeping mission. It does NOT represent an official United Nations order of precedence.*

United Nations Ribbon Placement

1. United States of America

* (Silver Life Saving Medal)

	Decoration (Bronze Star)	
Decoration Non-Military*	Unit Award (Navy)	Good Conduct Medal (Navy)
Service Award (Vietnam Service)	Foreign Decoration (RVN Gal. Cross)	Foreign Unit Award (RVN Civil Actions)
U.N. Medal (SEE NOTE 2)**	Foreign Service (RVN Campaign)	Marksmanship Award (Navy)

2. Canada

5

	Order (Order of Canada)	Decoration (Medal of Bravery)	
War Medal (Gulf & Kuwait Medal)	Service Award (Special Service Medal)	**U.N. Medal** (UNIIMOG)**	**U.N. Medal** (UNIKOM)**
U.N. Medal (UNMIH)**	Coronation Medal (Queen Elizabeth II)	Long Service Medal (Canadian Forces Dec'n)	Marksmanship Medal (Queen's Medal)

3. United Kingdom

	Order of Knighthood Royal Victorian Order)		
Decoration (Military Cross)	Gallantry Medal (Dist. Conduct Medal)	War Medal (South Atlantic Medal)	**U.N. Medal** (UNTAG)**
War Medal (Persian Gulf Medal)	**U.N. Medal** (UNAMIR)**	Jubilee/Coronation (Elizabeth II Jubilee)	Long Service Medal (RN Auxiliary Services)

NOTES:

1. United Nations awards are denoted above by a double asterisk (**).
2. Represents service with UNOSOM, (first ribbon awarded) and two subsequent United Nations peace keeping missions
3. The above ribbon displays do not represent the awards of any specific or typical individual. They merely illustrate placement of United Nations awards with reference to other unique award types and or categories.

The Different United Nations Mlitary and Civilian Medals

United Nations has several different classes of peacekeeping medals that have evolved over the years. The most familiar one is the United Nations Medal awarded military personnel predominately for peacekeeping mission. It is synonymous with the campaign medals awarded military personnel by different countries as a symbol of an individual's participation in that particular event. Over the past 70 years a number of different United Nations awards have evolved to recognize special events in the service of peacekeeping for the United Nations.

While not the first medal the Dag Hammarskjöld Medal is perhaps the most significant award since it represents the ultimate sacrifice of one's life in the service of peacekeeping missions for the United nation. (See below)

Another relatively new award and very rare to date is the Captain Mbaye Diagne Medal for Exceptional Courage. (page 20)

The third type of peacekeeping medal is the United Nations first award and was originally designated The United Nations Service Medal, a name used to this day by many of the nations who fought in the war in spite of an administrative change in 1961 to the name: The United Nations Korean Medal. (page 22)

The fourth type of United Nations medal was the United Nations Emergency Force Medal. Which has been awarded twice both times for services in the Sinai Peninsula. (page 25-26)

The fifth type of medal is the United Nations Headquarters service Medal which is awarded to military staff officers serving in the New York United Nations Headquarters to assist with the planning and implementation of new peacekeeping missions (page 106).

The sixth unique United Nations medal is the United Nations Medal for Special Service which recognizes military personnel and civilian police serving the United Nations in capacities other than established peacekeeping missions and the United Nations Headquarters (page 107).

The most well-known and awarded United Nations Medal is the United Nations Medal and for over 70+ years it has been awarded with differnt ribbon variations for each peacekeeping missions. Examples of the United Nations Medal are shown starting on page 27.

The Dag Hammarskjöld Medal

The United Nations awards the Dag Hammarskjöld Medal as a posthumous award to military personnel, police, or civilians who died serving in UN peacekeeping operations. The UN medal is named for Dag Hammarskjöld, , who died in a plane crash in Zambia in September 1961 while serving as Secretary-General of the United Nations.

The Dag Hammarskjöld Medal is made of clear egg-shaped glass, embossed with United Nations logo with the English and French inscription "The Dag Hammarskjöld Medal. In the Service of Peace". The Presentation medal is engraved with the name and date of death of the recipient.

The first three Dag Hammarskjöld Medals recipients were awarded to the next of kin of Dag Hammarskjöld, René de Labarrière (killed by a land mine in Palestine in 1948), and Folke Bernadotte (assassinated in Jerusalem by Jewish extremists in September 1948) in 1998.

Currently the award is presented to military, police, or civilian personnel who lose their lives during service with a peacekeeping operation under the operational control and authority of the United Nations. UN personnel are not eligible for the award if their death was from misconduct or criminal acts. While the medal was established on 1 January 2001 it may be awarded back to 1948 for individuals who meet the qualifications. The actual medal is presented to the next of kin whenever possible.

In 2001, the UN began awarding medals each month for the UN peacekeepers who had been killed between 1948 and 2001. Beginning in 2002 an annual medal ceremony is held on 29 May, International Day of United Nations Peacekeepers, for those who were killed in UN peacekeeping operations the previous year. In 2009, the medal was awarded to the 132 UN peacekeepers who were killed in 2008. Each year on Peacekeeper's Day, the medal is also awarded to any Member State who has lost one or more military or police peacekeepers at a ceremony at UN HQ.

In 2014, the Security Council created "the Captain Mbaye Diagne Medal for Exceptional Courage" for award to United Nations military, police, civilian personnel and associated personnel who demonstrate exceptional courage, in the face of extreme danger, while fulfilling their mission mandate or in the service of humanity and the United Nations."

The Captain Mbaye Diagne Medal, the Dag Hammarskjöld Medal and the United Nations Medal are the three United Nations awards presented to persons who have participated in the international humanitarian, military or police UN Mission. The medal is named after Mbaye Diagne, a Senegalese Captain and Military Observer of the United Nations in Rwanda, who was killed in Rwanda in 1994. The medal is awarded to persons who have shown extraordinary courage in an extremely dangerous situation while participating in a UN mission.

The front of the gold-coloured medal is the emblem of the United Nations with the words "United Nations, Exceptional Courage". The reverse of the medal is inscibed "Captain Mbaye Diagne Medal, in the Service of Peace". The ribbon is light blue with three gold stripes. The first award was presented to Captain Diagne's wife.

Captain Mbaye Diagne, a Senegalese Captain and Military Observer of the United Nations was awarded the National Order of the Lion by the Senegal government in addition to His UN award.

a. United Nations Korean Medal
(English Language Version)

b. United Nations Korean Medal
(Unofficial French Version)

United Nations Korean Medal

The UN's first award was originally designated *The United Nations Service Medal*, a name used to this day by many of the nations who fought in the war in spite of an administrative change in 1961 to *The United Nations Korean Medal*. The award dates from October, 1950, approximately three months after the outbreak of hostilities on the Korean Peninsula, when a petition was circulated in the United Nations General Assembly calling for the establishment of a "distinguishing ribbon or other insignia" for those who had "....participated in Korea in the defence of the principles of the Charter of the United Nations." The proposal was adopted in December of that year and formal regulations governing the design and wear of the medal were prescribed in 1951.

As enacted, the medal was defined as being of bronze alloy, round in form and 1.4 inches in diameter with one side depicting the emblem of the United Nations and the reverse bearing the inscription: FOR SERVICE IN DEFENCE OF THE PRINCIPLES OF THE CHARTER OF THE UNITED NATIONS. The ribbon was also delineated and is fully described later in this text. The eligibility requirements for the award and the regulations for its wear were also defined.

However, the most interesting portion of the regulations had to do with the option to strike the medal and the associated clasp in the native languages of the participating countries. As a result, the medal has been seen in 13 separate versions including two different types in Spanish, two in French and an unofficial issue in Tagalog, the language of The Philippines. This situation had not been seen in medallic circles since the World War I Victory Medal was issued with no fewer than 14 separate-language versions.

The two examples pictured at left are (a.) the English version, by far the most awarded (2,760,000 to nine participating countries) and (b.) the alternate French version which may be an unofficial copy. The remaining 11 variants are pictured on on the next pages.

Even in the medal field, the UN is not immune to confusion (admittedly minor in nature). Official UN documents list Danish, Sanskrit and Swedish as three of the languages used on the medal. However, a number of authoritative sources state that the Danes and Swedes accepted the English language version of the medal and no known example of the medal in Sanskrit exists.

KOREA - United Nations Korean Service

The ribbon is designed with a United Nations blue background and a series of white stripes across its width. These are the basic colors of the United Nations.

Gold plated verison
of Medal

Country/Location	Korea
Dates	June 1950 to July 1953
Countries Participating	(19) Australia, Belgium, Canada, Colombia, Ethiopia, France, Greece, Luxembourg, Netherlands, New Zealand, Philippines, South Korea, Thailand, Turkey, Union of South Africa, United Kingdom, United States (plus Denmark and Italy which provided medical support)
Maximum Srength	(approx): 1,000,000 (UN & South Korea combined)
Current Strength	NA
Fatalities	(approx): Korea: 415,000, U.S.: 55,000, Other UN: 3,100
Medal Number	NA
CLASP(S)	None

MANDATE: No formal mandate was ever proclaimed by the United Nations owing to the very unique nature of the UN involvement in Korea. It is not considered a peace-keeping operation since it did not fulfill the three basic definitions governing such an activity: it was not under the direct control of the United Nations, it was not based upon the consent of all of the disputants and the action used excessive amounts of force.

BACKGROUND: The peninsular nation of Korea was recognized as an independent nation by the treaty that ended the Sino-Japanese war of 1894-95, but was forcibly annexed by Japan in 1910, remaining in that situation until the end of World War II. As one of the conditions to bring Russia into the war against Japan, however, the nation was to be partitioned into two portions along the 38th parallel with Russian and U.S. troops occupying the north and south sections respectively. In 1948, as the Republic of South Korea was being proclaimed and trying to establish their first democratic government, the Democratic People's Republic of (North) Korea was being organized into a militant regime and being heavily armed by the Soviet Union. The withdrawal of U.S. forces in 1949 seemed to send a clear signal to the North that the way was now ready for an unopposed advanced into South Korea that would reunite the country under communist rule.

As a result, on 25 June 1950, 60,000 North Korean troops, backed by armor and artillery, crossed the 38th parallel in a massive invasion which was initially unopposed and soon threatened to engulf the entire country. World reaction was unusually swift and the UN Security Council met almost immediately to ponder this new threat to peace and issued a cease-fire proclamation to North Korea, which was totally ignored. Within two days, the UN adopted a resolution recommending that the member nations form a unified command and send troops to Korea to restore peace. To that end, General Douglas MacArthur, hero of the Pacific fighting in World War II was appointed overall UN commander and the participating nations rushed men and matériel to stop the communist advance.

Once the original invasion thrust was stopped at the Pusan perimeter, UN forces took the initiative with a brilliant landing behind enemy lines at Inchon, followed by a series of lightning attacks through the peninsula which cut off thousands of North Korean troops, recaptured the capital city of Seoul and moved well past the 38th parallel into the territory of the North. As the war seemed to be drawing to its conclusion, a surprise attack was launched by the forces of The People's Republic of China when they sent four fully-equipped armies across the Yalu River. The results were quite staggering to the UN forces as they went from a slow advance to full retreat under dreadful winter conditions. The UN lines eventually held and straightened at the 38th parallel and years of stalemate followed while truce talks dragged on. A truce agreement was finally signed in July 1953, ending a war which had caused nearly 3,500,000 casualties on all sides in three years of bloody warfare.

United Nations Korean Medal Variants

a. United Nations Korean Service Medal (English Version)

Awarded to:
Australia, Canada, Denmark, New Zealand, Norway, Philippines, Sweden, United Kingdom, Union of South Africa, United States

Bar: KOREA
Number: 2,760,000

b. United Nations Korean Service Medal (Amharic Version)

Awarded to:
Ethiopia

Bar:
KOREA
(in Amharic)

Number:
5,650

c. United Nations Korean Service Medal (Dutch Version)

Awarded to:
The Netherlands

Bar:
KOREA

Number:
5,800

d. United Nations Korean Service Medal (Standard French Version)

Awarded to:
Belgium, Canada (French-speaking) France and Luxembourg

Bar:
COREE

Number:
16,900

e. United Nations Korean Service Medal (Greek Version)

Awarded to:
Greece

Bar:
KOREA
(in Greek characters)

Number:
9,000

f. United Nations Korean Service Medal (Italian Version)

Awarded to:
Italy

Bar:
COREA

Number:
135

United Nations Korean Medal Variants

g. United Nations Korean Service Medal (Korean Version)

Awarded to:
South Korea

Bar:
KOREA (in Korean characters)

Number:
1,225,000

h. United Nations Korean Service Medal (Spanish Version)

Awarded to:
Colombia

Bar:
KOREA

Number:
1,300

i. United Nations Korean Service Medal (Tagalog Version)

Awarded to:
Philippines
(*unofficial copy*)

Bar:
KOREA

Number:
Unknown

j. United Nations Korean Service Medal (Thai Version)

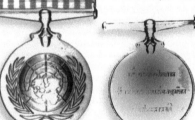

Awarded to:
Thailand

Bar:
KOREA (in Thai characters)

Number:
10,650

k. United Nations Korean Service Medal (Turkish Version)

Awarded to:
Turkey

Bar:
KORE

Number:
33,700

The Turkish Medal is normally seen with a plain, dark red ribbon rather than the "standard" United Nations Korean Ribbon. Owing to many centuries of political strife, economic rivalries and bitter warfare with their age-old enemy, Greece, the Turks refused to wear a medal whose ribbon they perceived as containing the colors of the Greek flag.

The final commentary on the United Nations Korean Medal has to do with old national animosities which never seem to die, even when the two countries are fighting on the same side in a war. The Turkish version of the medal is worn with a plain, dark red ribbon since the Turks would not wear the UN Korean medal ribbon, (light blue and white) the colors of Greece, their centuries-old adversary.

First United Nations Emergency Force Medal UNEF I

UNEF I: The sand/buff colored background symbolizes the Sinai Desert while the center band of light blue characterizes the United Nations. The two thin lines towards the edge represent the general area with the dark blue symbolizing the Suez Canal and the green for the Nile Valley.

United Nations Emergency Force Medal I

This is the most unique medal in the annals of the United Nations since it was only used for a single mission and had no variants in language or design. Prior to the establishment of the United Nations Medal, the well-accepted philosophy of "one medal for one mission" was firmly in place. The first two UN operations (e.g.: Korea and UNTSO) had produced distinctive medals so it came as no surprise when a separate medal was authorized for the UN troops who supervised the cessation of hostilities and withdrawal of foreign troops from the Suez Canal. In 1956, to maintain the peace which brought the end of the Suez Crisis the United Nations Emergency Force was established. This was the first Peacekeeping operation of the United Nations. Troops from Brazil, Canada, Colombia, Denmark, India, Norway, Sweden and Yugoslavia who completed ninety days of service with the UNEF were awarded the United Nations Emergency Force Medal. The mission lasted from November 1956 until June 1967.It is unique from other United Nations Medals in that instead of saying UN on the obverse, it says UNEF. Subsequent missions did not use the missions abbreviation on its medals.

The medal's obverse is quite similar to the UN Korean Medal with the addition of the curved letters, UNEF atop the "World-in-a-Wreath" symbol and a reverse containing the inscription, IN THE SERVICE OF PEACE in English (and only in English).

Secretary-General Dag Hammarskjold inspects UNEF's Brazilian Battalion, Rafah, Egypt, 1958.   UN Photo

UNEF I - First United Nations Emergency Force

UNEF I: *The sand/buff colored background symbolizes the Sinai Desert while the center band of light blue characterizes the United Nations. The two thin lines towards the edge represent the general area with the dark blue symbolizing the Suez Canal and the green for the Nile Valley.*

Country/Location	Egypt, Israel (Sinai Peninsula)
Dates	November 1956 to June 1967
Countries Participating	10) Brazil, Canada, Colombia, Denmark, Finland, India, Indonesia, Norway, Sweden, Yugoslavia
Maximum Srength	6,073 military observers (1957)
Strength at Withdrawal	3,378
Fatalities	107
Medal Number	NA
CLASP(S)	None

MANDATE: While the madate of UNEF I was to secure and supervise the cessation of hostilities, including the withdrawal of the armed forces of France, Israel and the United Kingdom from Egyptian territory and, after the withdrawal, to serve as a buffer between the Egyptian and Israeli forces.

The second United Nations Emergency Forces (UNEF II) was established by the 1973 United Nations Security Council Resolution 340. The UN mandate was to supervise the ceasefire between Egyptian and Israeli forces at the end of Yom Kippur War (also known as the October War), and following of the agreement in 1974 and 1975, the UN forces were to supervise the redeployment of Egyptian and Israeli forces and man and control the buffer zones established under the ceasefire agreements.

BACKGROUND: Although one outcome of the first Arab-Israeli war in 1948-49 was to be a peace treaty, a number of years had gone by and no such document was forthcoming. In the interim, Egypt had declared its sovereignty from years of British rule and an uprising that was led by senior army generals had deposed King Farouk, declaring the country an independent republic.

In October 1956, Egypt, Jordan and Syria combined their armed forces under Egyptian President Gamal Abdel Nasser command, setting off a lightning attack by Israel's military forces against Egypt. A secondary effect occurred when Britain and France, still reeling from Nasser's seizure of the Suez Canal, joined in the attack and in nine days had completed the occupation of the entire Sinai, Suez and had opened the Gulf of Aqaba.

The United Nations immediately attempted to take action within the Security Council but vetoes by both France and Great Britain had blocked any action. However, the General Assembly was able, within days, to institute a cease-fire among the disputants, arrange a swift withdrawal of all foreign forces and establish UNEF I, the First United Nations Emergency Force. In an action which was to be repeated many times in the future, military advisors/observers from the existing UNTSO operation were utilized for the new task. The UNEF operation was terminated just prior to the Six-Day War. The disengagement agreement was completed on February 5th, when the area south of Little Bitter Lake was turned over by the United Nations Emergency Force (UNEF) to the Egyptian forces. Sixteen hours earlier, the same area had been handed over to UNEF by the Israeli forces. The Israeli forces had moved further to the north and UNEF forces moved to an area where they had taken up positions and started patrolling in a temporary buffer zone approximately 35 kilometers long and 3 kilometers deep. UNEF, with the assistance of military observers of the U.N. Truce Supervision Organization in Palestine (UNTSO), and in the presence of Egyptian and Israeli liaison officers, also carried out an inspection to verify the redeployment of forces in the southernmost sector of the areas of limited armaments and forces.

An Indian paratrooper of the First Parachute battalion (PUNJAB) warns a civilian of the the Demarcation line between Egypt and Isreal 1958.

UNTSO - United Nations Medal

The ribbon is a United Nations blue background with a white stripe near each edge, the basic colors of the United Nations.

United Nations Medal (Peace Keeping)

The original UNTSO medal was awarded for the next few UN field operations (UNOGIL, ONUC) but it soon became obvious that a truly unique honor was needed for each mission. However, the costs involved in designing and issuing new medals for each mission, particularly those involving a relatively small number of personnel, could be prohibitive. The decision was made, therefore, to standardize the actual medal but equip each newly-authorized award with its own, individually-designed ribbon. This practice was formalized in 1966, when the Secretary-General established the so-called United Nations Medal as the standard award for all UN participants in its peace-keeping efforts.

As officially issued, the United Nations Medal is, once again, bronze in color and 1.4 inches in diameter, bearing on the obverse, the representation of the UN symbol surmounted by the straight letters UN, both in bas-relief. On the reverse, the expression, IN THE SERVICE OF PEACE has been perpetuated in bas-relief from previous designs.

A United Nations Medal is an international decoration awarded by the United Nations (UN) to the various world countries members for participation in joint international military and police operations such as peacekeeping, humanitarian efforts, and disaster relief. The medal is ranked in militaries and police forces as a service medal. The United Nations awarded its first medal during the Korean War (1950-53). Since 1955, many additional United Nations medals have been created and awarded for participation in various United Nations missions and actions around the world.

The most common United Nations medal is the standard UN decoration known simply as the United Nations Medal. Most countries bestow this award for any action in which a member of the military participated in a joint UN activity.

In situations where a service member participated in multiple UN operations, service stars, campaign clasps, or award numbers are authorized as attachments to the United Nations Medal. These devices vary depending on the regulations of the various armed forces.

The UN has authorised the award of numerals to be attached to the medal ribbon. The qualification for these numerals is not to indicate the number of campaigns served in, but rather the number of qualifying periods of service. Which are counted as 180 days after the initial qualifying period of 90 days if the service is performed as 270 days consecutive. For two or more deployments, each deployment has to be at least 90 consecutive days each.

UN Photo

Chronological United Nations Peace-Keeping Operations

	Years	Ribbon bar	Operation	Operation area	
1	1948–		UNTSO	Middle East	page 30
2	1949–		UNMOGIP	India, Pakistan	page 31
3	1958		UNOGIL	Lebanon, Syria	page 32
4	1960–1964		ONUC	Congo	page 33
5	1962–1963		UNSF	West-Papua **and** Indonesia	page 34
6	1963–1964		UNYOM	Yemen	page 35
7	1964–		UNFICYP	Cyprus	page 36
8	**1965-1996**	No medal	**DOMREP**	Dominican Republic	page 37
9	1965–1966		UNIPOM	India, Pakistan	page 38
10	1973–1979		UNEF II	Egypt, Israel	page 39
11	1974–		UNDOF	Golan Heights	page 40
12	1978–		UNIFIL	Lebanon	page 42
13	1988–1991		UNIIMOG	Iraq, Iran	page 44
14	1988–1990		UNGOMAP	Afghanistan, Pakistan	page 45
15	1988–1991		UNAVEM I	Angola	page 46
16	1989–1990		UNTAG	Namibia	page 47
17	1989–1992		ONUCA	Central America	page 48
18	1991–2003		UNIKOM	Kuwait, Iraq	page 49
19	1991–		MINURSO	Western Sahara	page 50
20	1991–1995		UNAVEM II	Angola	page 51
21	1991–1995		ONUSAL	El Salvador	page 52
22	1991–1992		UNAMIC	Cambodia	page 53
23	1992–1995		UNPROFOR	Croatia and Bosnia Herzegovina during Yugoslav Wars	page 54
24	1992–1993		UNTAC	Cambodia	page 56
25	1992–1993		UNOSOM I	Somalia	page 57
26	1992–1994		ONUMOZ	Mozambique	page 58
27	1993–1995		UNOSOM II	Somalia	page 59
28	1993–1994		UNOMUR	Rwanda, Uganda	page 60
29	1993–2009		UNOMIG	Georgia	page 61
30	1993–1997		UNOMIL	Liberia	page 62
31	1993–1996		UNAMIR	Rwanda	page 63
32	1993–1996		UNMIH	Haiti	page 64
33	1994-1994	No medal	UNASOG	Aouzou Strip Observer	page 65
34	1994–2000		UNMOT	Tajikistan during Civil War	page 66
35	1995–1997		UNAVEM III	Angola	page 67

36	1995–1999		UNPREDEP	Macedonia	page 68
37	1995–1996		UNCRO	Croatia	page 69
38	1995–2002		UNMIBH	Bosnia-Herzegovina	page 70
39	1996–1998		UNTAES	Croatia	page 71
40	1996–1997		UNSMIH	Haiti	page 72
41	1996–2002		UNMOP	Croatia	page 73
42	1997		MINUGUA	Guatemala	page 74
43	1997–1999		MONUA	Angola	page 75
44	1997		UNTMIH	Haiti	page 76
45	1997–2000		MIPONUH	Haiti	page 77
46	1998		UNPSG	Croatia	page 78
47	1998–2000		MINURCA	Central African Republic	page 79
48	1998–1999		UNOMSIL	Sierra Leone	page 80
49	1999–		UNMIK	Kosovo	page 81
50	1999		UNAMET	East Timor	page 82
51	1999–2005		UNAMSIL	Sierra Leone	page 83
52	1999–2002		UNTAET	East Timor	page 84
53	1999–2010		MONUC	Democratic Republic of the Congo	page 85
54	2000–2001		MICAH	Haiti	page 87
55	2000–2008		UNMEE	Eritrea, Ethiopia	page 88
56	2002–2005		UNMISET	East Timor	page 89
57	2003-2018		UNMIL	Liberia	page 90
58	2003–2004		MINUCI	Ivory Coast	page 91
59	2004–2018		UNOCI	Ivory Coast	page 92
60	2004–2017		MINUSTAH	Haiti	page 93
61	2004–2006		ONUB	Burundi	page 94
62	2005–2011		UNMIS	Sudan	page 95
63	2006–2012		UNMIT	East Timor	page 96
64	2007-2020		UNAMID	Sudan	page 97
65	2007–2010		MINURCAT	Central African Republic, Chad	page 98
66	2010–		MONUSCO	Democratic Republic of the Congo	page 99
67	2011–		UNISFA	Sudan	page 100
68	2011–		UNMISS	South Sudan	page 101
69	2012-		UNSMIS	Syria	page 102
70	2013–		MINUSMA	Mali	page 103
71	2014–		MINUSCA	Centeral African Republic	page 104
72	2015-2019		MINUJUSTH	Haiti	page 105
73	1974–		UNHQ	Service in the UN Hqs	page 106
74	1994		UNSSM	UN Special Service	page 107

1. The United Nations Missions

UNTSO - United Nations Truce Supervision Organization

UNTSO   The ribbon is a United Nations blue background with a white stripe near each edge, the basic colors of the United Nations.

Gold plated verison of Medal

Country/Location	Palestine/Israel
Dates	June 1948 to present
Countries Participating	Argentina, Australia, Austria, Belgium,Bhutan, Canada, Chile, China, Denmark, Estonia, Fuji, Finland, France, Gambia,Ireland, Italy, Myanmar, Netherlands, New Zealand, Norway, Poland,Sweden, Switzerland, United States, USSR (Major) **Maximum Srength 572** military observers (1948)
Current Strength	400 plus (All personnel)
Fatalities	50
Medal Number	1
CLASP(S)	**CONGO, UNGOMAP, OSGAP**

MANDATE: Established in 1948 to assist the UN Mediator and Truce Commission in supervising the truce observance in Palestine. Since then, UNTSO has performed various tasks, including supervision of the 1949 General Armistice Agreements and observation of the cease-fire in the Suez Canal area and the Golan Heights following the June 1967 Arab-Israeli war. At present, UNTSO assists and cooperates with the United Nations Disengagement Observer Force (UNDOF- see page 50) and the United Nations Interim Force in Lebanon (UNIFIL- page 52) in the performance of their tasks. UNTSO observer groups are stationed in Beirut and the Sinai Desert.

BACKGROUND: This was the first observer mission of the United Nations and, chronologically speaking, is the longest-running. It was formed in 1948 as a step towards the establishment

The observers and the United Nations flag became well known to the children in Palestine. UN Photo

and maintenance of a cease-fire during the first Arab-Israeli conflict. In 1947, the United Nations voted to partition Palestine, previously maintained by the British as a League of Nations mandate, into separate Arab and Jewish states. When British forces withdrew from Palestine, the Jewish settlers of the region promptly declared their independence and proclaimed the formation of the new state of Israel. Reaction within the Arab world was instantaneous and, within days, hostilities broke out between the new nation and the Arab states of Egypt, Jordan, Syria and Lebanon. In early 1948, a number of attempts were made to get the warring factions to agree to a cease-fire but initial efforts met with little or no success while major battles were being fought over large portions of disputed territory. However, as the tide of battle turned in favor of the Israelis and their forces now at the gates of the capital city of Jerusalem, both sides finally agreed to a truce to be supervised by the UN and its new entity, the United Nations Truce Supervision Organization (UNTSO). This coalition of volunteers, representing a number of member nations, was supervised by the United Nations Mediator, and included amongst its numbers the first group to be designated as military observers, a role that would be repeated many times in the coming years.

SUBSEQUENT ACTIVITIES: Since the establishment of UNTSO, there have been four additional full-scale wars associated with the Arab-Israeli conflict, all of which saw the establishment of United Nations peace-keeping operations in the region. Of these, three are still active; the overall UNTSO operation, the disengagement observer force in Syria and the Golan Heights (UNDOF) and the peace-keeping force in southern Lebanon (UNIFIL). The other two operations, the first and second UN Emergency Forces (UNEF and UNEF II) were mounted in the Egypt-Israel sector and have since been terminated. In addition, the UNTSO command was also called upon to provide manpower assistance to other UN operations in the Congo (ONUC) and Afghanistan/ Pakistan (UNGOMAP, OSGAP).

2. UNMOGIP - United Nations Military Observer Group in India and Pakistan

UNMOGIP: The ribbon: The wide central band in various shades of green represents the Himalayan Range and the Kashmir Valley and the white stripes flanking the green represent the snow-capped mountains. There are two bands of United Nations blue at the ribbon edges.

Country/Location	India, Pakistan (Jammu & Kashmir)
Dates	January 1949 to present
Countries Participating	(15) Australia, Belgium, Canada, Chile, Denmark, Ecuador, Finland, Italy, Korean Republic, Mexico, New Zealand, Norway, Sweden, United States, Uruguay
Maximum Srength	102 military observers (1965)
Current Strength	116 (2020)
Fatalities	11 (2020)
Medal Number	2
CLASP(S)	None

MANDATE: The United Nations Military Observer Group in India & Pakistan (UNMOGIP) was formed to negotiate and, subsequently, to supervise a cease-fire arranged in the disputed area of the State of Jammu and Kashmir.

BACKGROUND: After a century of British rule on the Indian subcontinent, India's independence movement came to full fruition at the end of World War II. It was the fervent wish of most prominent spokesmen in the early struggle for independence (Gandhi, Nehru, etc.) that a free India should embrace all of its ethnic elements in the formation of a new government. However, the leaders of the Moslem population, the largest minority, feared and mistrusted the Hindus and were adamant in their refusal to participate in any all-India government.

As a result, in August 1947, after the cessation of the British Raj in India, the two independent nations of India and Pakistan were created as homes for their indigenous Hindu and Moslem populations respectively. As part of the Independence Act of 1947, however, the State of Jammu and Kashmir could choose the country to which it wished to be allied, since it lay directly between the two new countries and the two religious factions were split almost equally within its borders. However, the matter of alliance soon became a matter of dispute between the two nations and extensive fighting broke out later that year.

In the 14-month war that ensued, the British-trained Indian army badly mauled both the Moslem tribesmen who lived in the province as well as Pakistani regulars who were sent to support them. Towards the end of 1948, in an act designed to gain additional UN cognizance over the conflict, Pakistan appealed to the United Nations Security Council, complaining that India was sending reinforcements across the border to conduct raids against the positions of the Azad (Free) Kashmir movement. In response to this request, a military advisor and a cadre of military advisors were appointed and dispatched to the subcontinent with instructions to observe the existing situation and propose methods of achieving a cease-fire in the region. As a result, a number of new recommendations were formulated which included proposals for a cessation of any further troop reinforcements, a formal truce agreement and a plebiscite to be held in the near future to determine the province's future once and for all. By the time these proposals were ratified by both parties on 1 January 1949, (the so-called "Karachi Agreement") India held nearly two-thirds of Kashmir. Subsequently, a number of UN efforts were made to arrange a demilitarization of Kashmir as a first step towards a plebiscite but neither India nor Pakistan would agree on terms for a planned withdrawal of forces. Amazingly, the tenuous cease-fire did hold until 1965 when further outbreaks of fighting involving the Rann of Kutch at the southern end of the two countries led to formation of the United Nations India/Pakistan Observer Mission (UNIPOM-). However, UNMOGIP is still active to this date.

Meeting between Indian and Pakistani officers and members of the UN Military Observer Group. UN Photo

3. UNOGIL - United Nations Observation Group in Lebanon

UNOGIL: The ribbon is a United Nations blue background with a white stripe near each edge, the basic colors of the United Nations (the same ribbon as UNTSO).

Country/Location	Lebanon, Syria
Dates	June to December 1958
Countries Participating	(20) Afghanistan, Argentina, Burma, Canada, Ceylon, Chile, Denmark, Ecuador, Finland, India, Indonesia, Ireland, Italy, Nepal, Netherlands, New Zealand, Norway, Peru, Portugal, Thailand
Maximum Srength	591 military observers
Current Strength	0
Fatalities	None
Medal Number	3
CLASP(S)	None

MANDATE: To ensure that there was no illegal infiltration of personnel or supply of arms or other matériel across the Lebanese borders.

BACKGROUND: In May 1958, an armed rebellion broke out in Lebanon when the then President, Camille Chamoun, sought legislation that would change the Lebanese Constitution to enable him to run for, and be elected to, another term in office. Owing to the country's ethnic and religious make-up, convention at that time was for the President to be a Maronite Christian and the prime minister a Moslem. Although the post of President was already the more important office, Chamoun was seeking to consolidate and escalate his own power and that of the Christians.

The disturbances originated in the predominantly Moslem city of Tripoli, spread to the capital city of Beirut and to the northern areas near the Syrian border and soon escalated into a full-scale civil war. In a classic case of seeking to further their own agenda in the already volatile area, it soon became obvious that Syria, now part of the United Arab Republic, was lending her considerable support to the Moslem cause. Such efforts started with the covert transportation of large quantities of arms and ammunition to rebels in Lebanon and culminated in the infiltration of a significant number of armed Syrian military personnel into the beleaguered country.

In May 1958, the Lebanese government requested an urgent meeting of the United Nations Security Council to present its complaints against Syria's intervention in their internal affairs. Before they could act, however, the government of Iraq requested and received a postponement to permit the League of Arab States to find a settlement. This effort went for naught, however, and the matter was finally brought to the UN in early June.

As the result of the UN meetings, and with the agreement of both the Lebanese and Syrian governments, the UNOGIL peace-keeping mission was established. In a short period, the international observer group of observers was deployed along the Syrian border. Observation posts, frequent ground patrols, aerial reconnaissance and evaluation teams were also established.

Complications arose in July 1958 when the King of Iraq was overthrown by a military coup d'état and President Chamoun appealed to the United States to intervene. In response, a U.S. Marine detachment was sent but their activities were limited to coastal areas and their influence was minimal. Similarly, the government of Jordan asked Great Britain to send troops to protect its territory and citizens from external threats.

Finally, President Chamoun relented on his desire for a second term in office and a candidate acceptable to both religious factions, General Fuad Chehab, was elected. As the turbulence wound down, foreign troops were removed and UNOGIL was terminated in Nov. 1958.

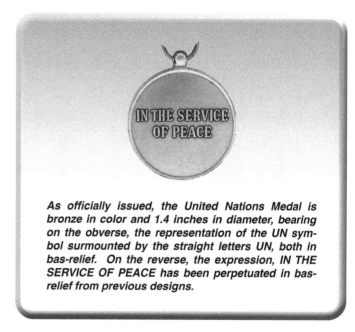

As officially issued, the United Nations Medal is bronze in color and 1.4 inches in diameter, bearing on the obverse, the representation of the UN symbol surmounted by the straight letters UN, both in bas-relief. On the reverse, the expression, IN THE SERVICE OF PEACE has been perpetuated in bas-relief from previous designs.

4. ONUC - United Nations Operation in the Congo

ONUC: Originally, the UNTSO ribbon, was awarded with the clasp, CONGO, affixed. In 1963, the existing ribbon was issued, containing a broad center band of green, representing hope for the new nation as well as the Congo Basin. The green center is flanked with light blue and white edge stripes symbolic of the United Nations' efforts.

Country/Location	Republic of Congo (now Zaire)
Dates	July 1960 to June 1964
Countries Participating	(30) Argentina, Austria, Brazil, Burma, Canada, Ceylon, Denmark, Ethiopia, Ghana, Guinea, India, Indonesia, Iran, Ireland, Italy, Liberia, Malaysia, Mali, Morocco, Netherlands, Nigeria, Norway, Pakistan, Philippines, Sierra Leone, Sudan, Sweden, Tunisia, United Arab Republic, Yugoslavia
Maximum Srength	19,828 military observers (1961)
Current Strength	0
Fatalities	250
Medal Number	Originally 1, then 4
CLASP(S)	**CONGO** worn with medal 1. When medal 4 was adopted, the bar was discontinued.

MANDATE: Initially, to ensure the withdrawal of Belgian forces, to assist the government in maintaining law and order and to provide technical assistance. The function of ONUC was subsequently modified to include maintaining the territorial integrity and political independence of the Congo, preventing the occurrence of civil war and securing removal from the Congo of all foreign military, paramilitary and advisory personnel not under the United Nations Command, and all mercenaries.

BACKGROUND: The territory of central Africa known as the Belgian Congo (now Zaire) had been under the control of Belgium since the 1884-85 Conference of Berlin. Encompassing the greatest part of the Congo Basin in the heart of Africa, the country enjoyed an important strategic position and was exceptionally rich in minerals. In spite of the rise of independence movements that swept across Africa after the Second World War, Belgium's colonial policies provided the region with one of the highest standards of living on the continent. However, in the areas of political and educational advancement, they were totally inadequate and few Congolese advanced educationally beyond the secondary level and entered the political process.

In 1959, increasing disturbances forced the colonial administration to review the situation and major reforms were proposed which led, inevitably, to a treaty granting total independence. However, under its terms, the Belgian military maintained a strong presence via the 25,000 man Force Publique with an all-Belgian officer corps. Incensed over lack of promotion within this police force, a mutiny broke out in the Leopoldville garrison in July 1960, which soon spread to several other cities. The atrocities against Europeans that followed caused many Belgian administrators to flee the country resulting in the collapse of essential services within the country.

As disorders increased, the Belgian Government intervened and sent in troops to restore law and order and to protect its nationals. The new government of the Congo then appealed to the United Nations to send military aid "...to protect the national territory of the Congo against the present external aggression which is a threat to international peace". ONUC, the resulting United Nations mission, is, by far, the largest peace-keeping operation ever established by the United Nations in terms of its responsibilities, the size of the area encompassed and manpower involved. Within an area of two million square miles, a force of nearly 20,000 men at its peak, plus a sizable civilian operations group, had to deal with enormous external pressures, the secession of its richest province (Katanga), a constitutional crisis and a level of internal chaos unknown up to that point. Ultimately, however, the UN's efforts did succeed in reuniting the country, restoring internal order and establishing a stable government. The region was declared secure in June 1964 and, per the conditions of the mandate, both the military and civilian contingents were withdrawn.

A member of the Ethiopian contingent of the Force takes time out to play with a newly found little friend near his Company camp in Kamina. UN Photo.

5. UNSF - United Nations Security Force in West New Guinea
UNTEA - United Nations Temporary Executive Authority

UNSF-UNTEA: The basic ribbon is United Nations blue with three central stripes in the colors of dark green, white and light green. The dark green represents the jungle and the swampland, the white denotes the snow capped mountains and the pale green stands for the coral beaches of the region.

Country/Location	West Irian (West New Guinea)
Dates	October 1962 to April 1963
Countries Participating	(9) Brazil, Canada, Ceylon, India, Ireland, Nigeria, Pakistan, Sweden, United States
Maximum Srength	1,576 military observers (1963)
Current Strength	0
Fatalities	None
Medal Number	5
CLASP(S)	None

MANDATE: To maintain peace and security in the territory under the United Nations Temporary Executive Authority (UNTEA) established by agreement between Indonesia and The Netherlands.

BACKGROUND: As late as the 1930s, the world's major nations were riding the crest of a huge wave of wealth, resources and strategic locales provided by their overseas possessions. World War II, however, provided the catalyst that forced a drastic change in most of the world's colonial powers. Nowhere was this more evident than in South-East Asia where The Netherlands maintained its hold on their mineral-rich possessions in the Dutch East Indies. Even older than the British Empire, the Dutch had replaced the Portuguese as the major European

trade influence as far back as the 17th century and had secured territorial rights in Java in the mid-1700s and West New Guinea in 1828. However, as in many similar cases, the war gave rise to a nationalist movement which forced The Netherlands to cede its sovereignty to the new country of Indonesia in 1949. Unfortunately, the status of the western portion of New Guinea, known as West Irian, was left quite vague by the treaty. Indonesia claimed that the territory rightfully belonged to them and the Dutch maintained that the large number of Papuan inhabitants should be free to decide their own future.

The matter of sovereignty was brought to the attention of the United Nations General Assembly at various times between 1954 and 1961 but no resolutions were adopted and no further action was taken. However, the situation worsened in early 1962 when a large contingent of Indonesian paratroops landed in West Irian. These incursions continued sporadically over the next few months and eventually led to armed clashes with Dutch and local Papuan troops. In July of that year, when both sides finally indicated a willingness to discuss the worsening situation, the United Nations was able to arrange a cease-fire in advance of full-scale negotiations over the future status of the territory.

An agreement was reached by which the administration of the territory of West Irian was transferred to a new entity, the United Nations Temporary Executive Authority (UNTEA) while local populations determined their country of preference. Also created was a United Nations Security Force (UNSF) which assisted UNTEA in carrying out the General Assembly's mandate and supervised the creation of a viable, local police force. The transition to Indonesian control was marred by only a few minor incidents as Dutch officers and enlisted personnel were replaced by Indonesians and the Papuan Volunteer Corps was disbanded. For the most part, the transition went smoothly and UNTEA and UNSF operations were officially terminated in April 1963.

On December 31, 1962, the U.N. and Indonesian Flags were raised together in West New Guinea (West Irian). UN Photo.

6. UNYOM - United Nations Yemen Observation Mission

UNYOM: The center of the ribbon contains various shades of brown denoting the dry and rugged mountains of Yemen, the lighter shades of yellow and gold represent the desert and the light blue edge stripes stand for the United Nations. Sixty days of service were required to qualify for the award of the medal.

Country/Location	Yemen
Dates	July 1963 to Sept. 1964
Countries Participating	(11) Australia, Canada, Denmark, Ghana, India, Italy, Netherlands, Norway, Pakistan, Sweden, Yugoslavia
Maximum Srength	25 military observers & 164 military personnel in reconnaissance and supporting air units (1964)
Current Strength	0
Fatalities	None
Medal Number	6
CLASP(S)	None

MANDATE: To observe and certify the implementation of the disengagement agreement between Saudi Arabia and the United Arab Republic.

BACKGROUND: In the Middle East of the early 1960s, extreme pressures on the royal families still ruling Arab countries were to bring about changes in an area already famous for intrigue, fanaticism and political instability. With the formation of The United Arab States in 1958, it was hoped that the new union would restore some measure of security to the region. However, that strange alliance of intensely nationalistic Egypt, profoundly suspicious Syria and the Royal Kingdom of Yemen was doomed from its outset and was dissolved in 1961.

In 1962, a chain of events was set in motion that would significantly alter the situation in the little kingdom of Yemen for years to come. In September of that year, the reigning Imam (King) of Yemen died and was succeeded by his son, Imam Mohammed Al-Badr. Less than a week later, however, an army-inspired uprising deposed the new Imam and proclaimed the formation of the new Yemen Arab Republic. Given the well-known desire of President Gamal Nasser of Egypt to rid the Middle East of all west-leaning royal houses, it came as no surprise when the United Arab Republic recognized the new government within a few days. Following his overthrow, Imam Al-Badr managed to escape from the capital with his royal family and immediately organized the tribes inhabiting the northern portion of the country.

The major players wasted little or no time in choosing sides in the internal conflict. Great Britain, for example, was fully aware that the new state continued Yemen's long-standing claim of sovereignty over Britain's South Arabian Federation which included the Aden Protectorate. Egypt took the opportunity to pour as many as 40,000 men and massive amounts of supplies in to support the revolutionary government against the royalists. The United States found itself having to contend with another unstable Arab government uncomfortably close to its oil lifeline. Finally, the Kingdom of Saudi Arabia, fearing revolutionary soldiers and tanks behind every sand dune along the extended border between the two countries, dispatched large quantities of war matériel to the royalist-backed tribesman.

Recognizing the seriousness of the situation, King Hussein of Jordan brought the matter to the attention of the United Nations and Secretary-General U Thant undertook a peace initiative which eventually led to the formation of the United Nations Yemen Observer Mission (UNYOM) in 1963. The original hope was for a disengagement of internal forces, the total removal of all foreign troops in country and the elimination of all external sources of supply. Owing to the limited resources of UNYOM, extreme difficulties faced in country and its limitation to observation only, the mission was somewhat less than a success. However, an ensuing military stalemate and some level heads ultimately led to a resolution of the controversy and the mission was terminated in September 1964.

On June 11, 1963, the Security Council approved a United Nations Observation Mission in Yemen (UNYOM), for the purpose of "ensuring against any developments in that situation which might threaten the peace of the area". UN Photo.

7. UNFICYP - United Nations Peace-Keeping Force in Cyprus

UNFICYP: The ribbon is divided into three equal segments of light blue and white, the basic colors of the United Nations and its various peace-keeping operations. The bands are separated by narrow bands of dark navy blue symbolizing the Mediterranean Sea.

Country/Location	Cyprus
Dates	March 1964 to present
Countries Participating	Argentina, Australia, Austria, Canada, Denmark, Finland, Hungary, Ireland, New Zealand, Sweden, United Kingdom, Italy, India, Romania, Chile, Slovakia
Maximum Srength	6,411 military observers (1964)
Current Strength	1,009 (2020)
Fatalities	183 (2020)
Medal Number	7
CLASP(S)	None

MANDATE: To use its best efforts to prevent the recurrence of fighting and, as necessary, to contribute to the maintenance and restoration of law and order and a return to normal conditions. Since the hostilities of 1974, this has included supervising the cease-fire and maintaining a buffer zone between the lines of the Cyprus National Guard and of the Turkish and Turkish Cypriot forces.

BACKGROUND: The strategically-located island of Cyprus, lying just 40 miles off the coast of Turkey, has, since the 1960s, become the symbol of ancient hatreds so deep-seated and monumental in scope that not even the most fervent optimist can visualize an amicable solution. Since Greece gained its independence from the Ottoman Empire in 1829, there have been very few periods when true peace has reigned between the two neighbors and the wars of 1912 and 1919 did nothing to improve the situation. Even joint membership in the North Atlantic Treaty Organization (NATO) and participation in the Korean War on the same side have done little to heal the long-standing enmity between the two. It is this climate that has faced the United Nations since the late 1950s when strong nationalistic feelings emerged in the majority Greek population.

Cyprus had been an Ottoman province from 1571 to 1878 when administration of the island had been surrendered to Great Britain in return for its assistance during a war with Russia. In the intervening years, however, the ethnic make-up of the population had shifted dramatically, until, after World War II, the Turks made up only 18 percent of the population. It was in this atmosphere, much to the dismay of the Turkish nationals, that the Greek inhabitants began agitating for union with their mother country. In 1954, a guerilla war was launched by the Greeks against the British in order to hasten their withdrawal but agreements to grant full independence were not concluded until 1959. Although the accords appeared on their face to protect the rights of the Turkish minority, this was merely an illusion and fighting between the two communities broke out in 1963 and threatened to escalate into a full-scale war between the two mother nations.

After the failure of a number of international peace conferences, United Nations assistance was sought and the UNFICYP peace-keeping mission was created. The initial efforts of this mission were reasonably successful and, by 1967, a stable cease-fire was achieved but no talks had yet taken place to bring about a political settlement. The next few years saw some minor fighting and local tensions but the peace was seriously threatened in 1974 when the Cypriot National Guard, led by Greek Army officers, seized the government. The move was countered by Turkish forces which invaded and ultimately occupied forty percent of the island, effectively partitioning Cyprus into separate Greek and Turkish sectors. Although the Greek Army was fully mobilized, it did not intervene and the status quo exists to this day. The United Nations efforts to achieve a lasting settlement continue and UNFICYP is still active.

In the absence of a political settlement to the Cyprus problem, UNFICYP has remained on the island to supervise ceasefire lines, maintain a buffer zone, undertake humanitarian activities and support the good offices mission of the Secretary-General.

United Kingdom Forces recieve medals. UN Photo

8. DOMREP - Mission of the Representative of the Secretary-General in the Dominican Republic

NO MEDAL ISSUED

Country/Location	Dominican Republic
Dates	May 1965 to October 1966
Countries Participating	(3) Brazil, Canada, Ecuador
Maximum Srength	2 military observers
Current Strength	0
Fatalities	0
Medal Number	None
CLASP(S)	None

MANDATE: To observe the situation and to report on breaches of the cease-fire between the two de facto authorities in the Dominican Republic.

BACKGROUND: The internal strife which occurred in the Dominican Republic in 1965 seemed on its face to be a distant cousin of the constant turmoil experienced in similar Caribbean nations earlier in the twentieth century. A political crisis had developed when the existing government was overthrown by a military coup attempting to return former President Juan Bosch to office. The result was that two rival governments, each claiming to be the legal ruling authority, emerged during the first few weeks of the civil war. Given the volatility of the political situation, it came as no surprise when intense fighting broke out between the two factions, primarily in the capital city of Santo Domingo.

As in many previous situations, the new troubles were met by an age-old response to previous Western Hemisphere struggles, the intervention of the United States and the landing of armed troops. President Lyndon Johnson announced that a contingent of U.S. Marines had been dispatched to the Dominican Republic to protect U.S. interests and to escort American citizens to safety. However, President Johnson, ordered the troops to take no part in the actual fighting and notified the United Nations and the Organization of American States (OAS) of his actions in the hope that either organization would act to bring about the restoration of peace and normality. Initial efforts of the OAS to bring the warring sides to the bargaining table met with little or no success and, in a strange twist, some difficulties actually arose between OAS and UN representatives as each accused the other of interference in their efforts to achieve a cease-fire. But soon, with the assistance of a newly-formed Inter-American Peace Force (IAPF), a general cease-fire was arranged and the OAS generated a series of proposals which would lead to a political settlement. These included general elections within 6 to 9 months, general amnesty for the participants in the civil strife, surrender of all arms in the hands of civilians and establishment of a single provisional government.

However, things were not to be as simple as the basic plan. At various times during the next year, contingents of armed troops from both sides exchanged fire, not only with each other but also with IAPF forces. This resulted in many casualties, few tangible results and certainly no appreciable improvement in the search for a lasting peace and a stable government. Finally, after much concerted effort, the OAS Secretary-General was able to announce that national elections would be held on 1 June 1966. The balloting proceeded without major incident, the new government was installed and, by October 1966, both the United Nations observers and OAS military personnel were withdrawn.

The medal pictured above was designed and struck by the O.A.S. for participants in the Dominican Operation. However, it was never issued. It is commonly referred to as "the medal that never was".

9. UNIPOM - United Nations India-Pakistan Observation Mission

UNIPOM: The wide central band in various shades of green represents the Himalayan Range and the Kashmir Valley and the white stripes flanking the green represent the snow-capped mountains. There are two bands of United Nations blue at the ribbon edges. This is the same ribbon as the UNMOGIP operation,.

Country/Location	India, Pakistan (Kashmir)
Dates	September 1965 to March 1966
Countries Participating	Initially: (12) Australia, Belgium, Canada, Chile, Denmark, Finland, Ireland, Italy, Netherlands, New Zealand, Norway, Sweden. Then: (10) Brazil, Burma, Canada, Ceylon, Ethiopia, Ireland, Nepal, Netherlands, Nigeria, Venezuela
Maximum Srength	96 military observers (1965)
Current Strength	0
Fatalities	None
Medal Number	9
CLASP(S)	None

MANDATE: To supervise the cease-fire along the India/Pakistan border (except in the State of Jammu and Kashmir where UNMOGIP operated) and the withdrawal of all armed personnel to the positions held by them before 5 August 1965.

BACKGROUND: As previously described under the UNMOGIP operation (see pg. 31), the original dispute between India and Pakistan, while not satisfactorily concluded in early 1965, had at least settled down to a point of armed quiescence. However, relations between the two countries soon became strained owing to conflicting claims over the Rann of Kutch at the southern end of the border between the two countries. The situation steadily deteriorated as summer approached and military hostilities soon erupted on a large scale along the cease-fire line in Kashmir. The UNMOGIP observers were forced to conclude that the original cease-fire agreement of July 1949 had totally collapsed and peace could not be achieved until the disputants reached a political, vice military, solution.

The United Nations Security Council, ever mindful of the previous history of mindless slaughter of innocent civilians in the previous India/Pakistani war, moved quickly towards the cessation of hostilities and increased its efforts to bring the two factions to the bargaining table. Once that was accomplished, it was proposed to strengthen the UNMOGIP forces as quickly as possible to reestablish the previous truce lines. However, no true cease-fire was immediately realized and the fighting continued. By September, the hostilities had spread to the international border between India and West Pakistan and fears were mounting that all-out war was possible.

By this time, the Security Council had seen a number of demands for the discontinuation of hostilities go by the boards with little or no response. Local commanders had been persuaded

to restrain their troops but sporadic clashes still occurred with monotonous regularity. However, as the fighting wore down, the UN, once again proposed to reinforce its UNMOGIP operation and use its established machinery as the prime means of supervising the truce. In a change of policy, though, since the hostilities extended beyond the original Jammu-Kashmir cease-fire line, a separate administrative adjunct, the United Nations India/Pakistan Observer Mission (UNIPOM) was created to supervise the new area of dispute. To ensure that the previous operation was not compromised in any way, strength was not drawn from UNMOGIP but, instead, a force was created composed of participants from 10 different nations.

UNIPOM's mission was primarily to observe and report breaches of the cease-fire and then try to persuade local commanders to restore the truce. While they had no authority or power to force the cessation of firing, the situation steadily improved. Finally, by 1966, an amicable plan calling for the withdrawal of all forces back to the original 1949 Karachi Agreement lines of demarcation had been approved and implemented by the two nations and the UNIPOM mission was terminated.

UN Photo

10. UNEF II - Second United Nations Emergency Force

UNEF II : The ribbon bears a wide central band of a sand or buff colour symbolizing the Sinai Desert with two narrow dark blue lines through the middle, representing the Suez Canal. Two wide bars of UN blue appear at either end. Eligibility period was 90 days of service in the Mission.

Country/Location	Egypt (Suez Canal), Israel, (Sinai Peninsula)
Dates	1973 to July 1979
Countries Participating	(13) Australia, Austria, Canada, Finland, Ghana, Indonesia, Ireland, Nepal, Panama, Peru, Poland, Senegal, Sweden
Maximum Srength	6,973 military observers (1974)
Current Strength	0
Fatalities	51
Medal Number	10
CLASP(S)	None

MANDATE: To supervise the cease-fire between Egyptian and Israeli forces and, following the conclusion of the agreements of 18 January 1974 and 4 September 1975, to supervise the redeployment of Egyptian and Israeli forces and to man and control the buffer zones established under those agreements.

BACKGROUND: The political atmosphere in the Middle-East of the early 1970s had changed very little from the days of the first Arab-Israeli conflict. The most obvious transformation was the amount of terrain held by the State of Israel. The June 1967 War, in which Israel had wiped out major portions of the Arab air and armored forces in just six days, had also brought vast new territories under the Israeli flag. By 1973, the Arab leaders, still smarting from the humiliation and havoc wreaked by "the little upstarts in their midst" had conceived a plan designed, not only to recover the lands lost in previous conflicts, but to achieve the ultimate destruction of the State of Israel.

On 6 October, in a surprise move, Egyptian forces crossed the Suez Canal and had soon progressed far in advance of the United Nations (UNTSO) observation posts set up on the Canal's eastern bank. In a coordinated move, Syrian troops simultaneously attacked Israeli positions on the hotly-disputed Golan Heights. The combined Egyptian-Syrian thrusts could not have been better timed, coming as they did during Israel's celebration of their holiest of Holidays, the Day of Atonement. The Yom Kippur War, as it came to be known, had caught the Israelis with their guard down since most of the defenders were either at home or in synagogues observing the holiday in prayer and fasting.

The initial progress of the well-planned, dual-thrust attack on the little country was quite good, given the notable lack of success achieved by the Arabs during the previous wars in 1948, 1956 and 1967. However, the Israelis, bolstered by a massive resupply effort initiated by the United States, soon regained the initiative, stalemating the Syrians on the Golan Heights and forcing the Egyptians out of the Sinai Peninsula back to the eastern bank of the Suez Canal. At this point, the UN Security Council acceded to the request of the combatants to step into a situation which now threatened to involve the United States and the Soviet Union. It was easily the most dangerous threat to world peace since the Cuban Missile Crisis of October 1962.

To ease the situation, the UN established the second UN Emergency Force (UNEF II), initially drawing upon personnel from the existing UNTSO and UNFICYP operations for manpower and ultimately filling out its ranks from other member nations. Under the terms of the cease-fire agreements, UNEF II was responsible for monitoring the cease-fire and the ultimate withdrawal of Israeli forces from the Sinai Peninsula. With stability returned to the region, the mandate of UNEF II lapsed in 1979 and the operation was terminated.

The first elements of the new United Nations Emergency Force arrived in Cairo on October 26, 1973, the day after the adoption of the Security Council Resolution setting up the Force. The task of the Force (Austria, Canada, Finland, Ireland, Peru, Poland and Sweden) is to supervise the implementation of the Security Council resolution which "Demands parties return to the positions occupied by them at 1650 hours GMT on October 22, 1973". UN Photo.

On May 31, Israel and Syria signed an agreement to cease fire, separate their armies on the Golan Heights and repatriate wounded and other prisoners-of-war held by either side. A view of UNDOF Position HOTEL on the top of the 2,682 meter peak of Mt. Hermon, which was manned by members of the Austrian battalion. UN Photo.

11. UNDOF - United Nations Disengagement Observer Force

UNDOF: The ribbon contains a central stripe of UN blue with a red line down the middle representing the UN patrolled Area of Separation; two narrow stripes of black, representing the volcanic rock of the Golan region appear on either side with two narrow bands of white, symbolic of the snow on Mt. Hermon, outside these. At either end are wide bands of burgundy, symbolizing the purple haze at sunset and the native thistles of the Golan. Ninety days service is the qualifying time for award of the medal.

Country/Location	Israel, Syria (Golan Heights)
Dates	June 1974 to present
Countries Participating	(7) Austria, Canada, Finland, Iran, Japan, Peru, Poland
Maximum Srength	1,450 authorized
Current Strength	1,040 military observers (2020) assisted by personnel from UNTSO's Observer Group, Golan
Fatalities	54 (2020
Medal Number	11
CLASP(S)	UNGOMAP, OSGAP

MANDATE: To supervise the cease-fire between Israel and Syria; to supervise the disengagement of Israeli and Syrian forces, and to supervise the areas of separation and limitation, as provided in the Agreement on Disengagement between Israeli and Syrian forces of 31 May 1974.

BACKGROUND: At the end of the Yom Kippur War in October 1973, while calm was restored on the Egyptian/ Israeli front primarily through the efforts of UNEF II, no new peacekeeping effort had been undertaken on the Syrian front. The fighting had actually subsided on the Golan Heights at the time of the cessation of hostilities, but by that time Israeli (next page) forces had advanced well past the 1967 cease-fire lines and were encamped within a short distance of Damascus, the Syrian capital. It goes without saying that the tensions in the area were extremely high and, by March 1974, the situation had become increasingly unstable. United Nations military observers attached to the UNEF II operation set up temporary observation posts around the Israeli salient and the cease-fire observation effort was resumed.

However, in spite of the UN's efforts to stabilize the situation, a continuous stream of incidents occurred in the general area of the observers, usually involving artillery, mortar and automatic weapons fire. By the middle of May, the conditions had worsened further and the firing now involved tanks, rockets and fighter-bomber aircraft. Against this background, the U.S. Secretary of State undertook a mediation mission, which resulted in an Agreement on Disengagement between Israeli and Syrian forces in May 1974. The protocols necessary to carry out the terms of the agreement were signed in Geneva and the way was paved for the establishment of a new UN mission, the United Nations Disengagement Observer Force (UNDOF).

As in the past, initial staffing was to be drawn from the other UN observer missions in the area, UNEF II and UNTSO, with the ultimate manpower complement to come from the member nations. Cessation of the fighting took place as scheduled on 31 May and, in the first phase of the disengagement agreement, Israeli troops returned approximately 275 square kilometers to Syrian control. To forestall any unauthorized activity, the UN moved in immediately and established a new buffer zone to the east of the evacuated area.

The buffer zone is currently inhabited and is policed by Syrian authorities. There are several towns and villages within and bordering the zone, including the ruins of Quneitra. Land mines continue to pose a significant danger to UNDOF and the civilian population. The fact that the explosives have begun to deteriorate worsens the threat. Mine clearance is conducted by Austrian and Polish battalions, directed from the UNDOF headquarters

During the Syrian conflict, however, there were violations of the ceasefire with the escalation of military activity in the area of separation patrolled by UNDOF peacekeepers. On June 29, 2017, the Security Council unanimously adopted resolution 2361 (2017) renewing UNDOF's mandate until December 2017, and strongly condemned the use of heavy weapons by the Syrian armed forces and armed groups in the area of separation.. UNDOF operations continue to this day.

In accordance with the terms of the agreement, the Security Council immediately set up a UN Disengagement Observer Force (UNDOF) to supervise implementation of the agreement for an initial period of 6 months. The force became operational on June 6th. By June 26, 1974, the four phases of the disengagement agreement had been completed smoothly and on schedule and the new UN Force had taken up positions in a buffer zone extending from Mt. Hermon in the north of the Jordanian border in the south.

The force was made up of observers from the UN Truce Supervision Organization (UNTSO), which has been serving in the area since the truce of 1948, and Austrians, Peruvians and Canadians and Polish logistics personnel formerly serving with the UN Emergency Force (UNEF II) established in October 1973 to observe the cease fire between Israel and Egypt and supervise the disengagement of forces agreement reached by those countries in January 1974.

Members of the Israeli Armed Force (in the background) prepare to withdraw from their position on the highest peak (2814 m.) on Mt. Hermon in accordance with Phase 3 of the disengagement of forces agreement. Looking on are members of UNDOF forces. UN Photo.

12. UNIFIL - United Nations Interim Force in Lebanon

UNIFIL: The ribbon bears three equal bands of UN colour: blue, green and UN blue. The bands are separated by two equal sized white stripes, each bisected by a narrow red line. The colours represent the UN and Lebanese flags. The qualifying period of service to earn the medal is 90 days of service in the Mission.

Country/Location	Southern Lebanon
Dates	March 1978 to present
Countries Participating	(15) Canada, Fiji, Finland, France, Ghana, Iran, Ireland, Italy, Nepal, Netherlands, Nigeria, Norway, Poland, Senegal, Sweden
Maximum Srength	15,000 authorized
Current Strength	11,082 (2019) assisted by personnel from UNTSO's Observer Group, Lebanon
Fatalities	316 (2020)
Medal Number	12
CLASP(S)	UNGOMAP, OSGAP

MANDATE: To confirm the withdrawal of Israeli forces from southern Lebanon, to restore international peace and security and to assist the Government of Lebanon in ensuring the return of its effective authority in the area.Following the July/August 2006 crisis, the Council enhanced the Force and decided that in addition to the original mandate, it would, among other things, monitor the cessation of hostilities; accompany and support the Lebanese armed forces as they deploy throughout the south of Lebanon; and extend its assistance to help ensure humanitarian access to civilian populations and the voluntary and safe return of displaced persons.

Secretary-General Kurt Waldheim paid a brief visit to the Middle East for the purpose of discussing with the parties concerned and with the UN Commanders the implementation in all its parts of Security Council resolution 425 of March 19, 1978. At left is Major-General Emmanuel Alexander Erskin (Ghana), UNIFIL Commander, and at right is Colonel Vigar Aabek, Commander of the Norwegian battalion. UN Photo.

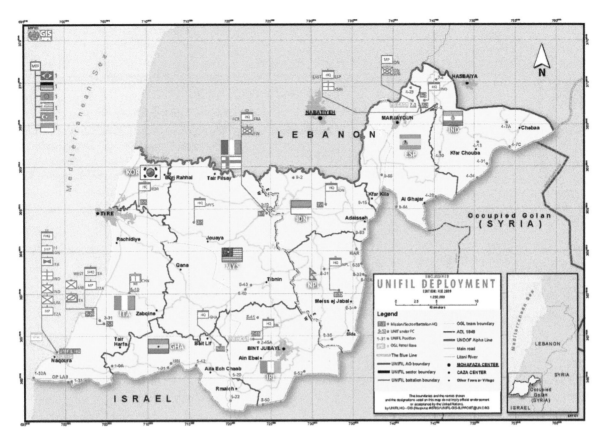

UNIFIL Deployment as of February 2018 UN Photo.

BACKGROUND: The civil war in Lebanon that had raged from 1975 to 1976 ended after all parties agreed upon the election of a new president and the formation of a new government. However, the new body found itself unable to bring the southern portion of Lebanon under government control. As a result, many clashes occurred between the local Christian militias in the south, which received support from Israel, and other leftist and Moslem factions supported by armed elements of the Palestine Liberation Organization (PLO). That organization was a dominant force in the area, establishing many bases in the region and launching commando raids against Israel. As had been its practice since creation of their own country, the Israelis always retaliated with fierce intensity.

In March 1978, a commando raid, for which the PLO took responsibility, took place near Tel Aviv resulting in a large number of casualties amongst the Israeli population. Instead of the usual attack on PLO position and camps by fighter-bombers, Israel retaliated by invading southern Lebanon and, within a few days had occupied most of the area south of the Litani River. In one of the classic ironies of history, the central Government of Lebanon vigorously protested the Israeli invasion since is was not responsible for the presence of the Palestinian bases in the south and, therefore, had no responsibility for the PLO raids. The United Nations responded by forming the United Nations Interim Force in Lebanon (UNIFIL) which supervised the Israeli withdrawal from the area between April and June of 1978.

All was not to remain calm in the area, however. In April 1982, as the result of repeated terrorist acts and rocket attacks upon civilian towns in northern Israel, the Israelis invaded southern Lebanon again, this time with two full mechanized divisions and full air and naval support. Under intense pressure from the UN and a multinational force sent to the area, a cease-fire was arranged and, simultaneously, 10,000 PLO fighters and 3,500 Syrian troops were evacuated. Soon thereafter, Israeli forces withdrew to a line south of Beirut.

The 2010 Israel–Lebanon border clash occurred on 3 August 2010. It was the deadliest incident along the border since the devastating 2006 Lebanon War. The UN force stationed in southern Lebanon urged "maximum restraint" following the clashes along the so-called Blue Line, a UN-drawn border separating Lebanon from Israel. UNIFIL peacekeepers were in the area where the clashes took place.

One former UNIFIL official explained that he has been in these situations before, and when the opposing sides are determined to shoot each other, there's nothing UNIFIL force can do. A former UNIFIL commander stated, concerning UNIFIL's action to preserve neutrality for both sides, that if UNIFIL forces intervene to protect IDF, for instance, UNIFIL will be accused by Hezbollah or the people of protecting the Israelis, and collaborating with the enemy. On the other side, if UNIFIL forces do the same with the Lebanese, Israel will accuse UNIFIL of collaborating with Hezbollah.

13. UNIIMOG - United Nations Iran-Iraq Military Observer Group

UNIIMOG: The ribbon has a broad central band of UN blue flanked on the left end by three equal stripes in green, white and red to represent the Iranian flag, and on the right end, by three equal stripes of red, white and black to represent the Iraqi flag. Ninety days of service in the Mission were required to qualify for the medal.

Country/Location	Iran, Iraq
Dates	August 1988 to February 1991
Countries Participating	(26) Argentina, Australia, Austria, Bangladesh, Canada, Denmark, Finland, Ghana, Hungary, India, Indonesia, Ireland, Italy, Kenya, Malaysia, New Zealand, Nigeria, Norway, Peru, Poland, Senegal, Sweden, Turkey, Uruguay, Yugoslavia, Zambia
Maximum Srength	400 military observers (1990)
Current Strength	--
Fatalities	1
Medal Number	13
CLASP(S)	None

MANDATE: To verify, confirm and supervise the cease-fire and the withdrawal of all forces to the internationally-recognized boundaries, pending a comprehensive settlement.

BACKGROUND: The conflict between Iran and Iraq, dating from the first outbreak of hostilities in 1980, took eight years before a significant United Nations effort could effect a measure of peace in the area. The initial dispute centered about the sovereignty of Shatt al-Arab, the navigable waterway which divides the two countries. After almost a year of intermittent skirmishing between the two countries, the situation deteriorated into open warfare when Iraqi fighter-bomber aircraft attacked a number of Iranian airfields, including the commercial facility at the capital city of Teheran. In retaliation, Iran launched heavy strikes at important targets inside of Iraq. The following weeks witnessed heavy ground fighting around the oil shipping ports on the Persian Gulf while Iraq launched attacks on the oil-producing

Above, Major General Slavko Jovic (Yugoslavia), Chief Military Observer of UNIIMOG, placing flowers on the casket at a funeral service for the first UNIIMOG casualty, a soldier who died of heatstroke. UN Photo.

province of Khuzistan. Although Iraq's army was driven back across their own border in 1982, the combatants could not be persuaded to discuss a settlement.

Further problems soon arose to further confuse an already complicated situation. In spite of intense United Nations peace initiatives, the conflict soon escalated into all-out war. Stories about thousands of Iranian soldiers charging in human wave attacks, the use of deadly chemical weapons by Iraq and inhumane treatment of prisoners-of-war by both sides filtered out of the area and made any form of settlement a distant dream. The war also expanded to the Persian Gulf in April 1984 with several attacks upon oil tankers, the laying of mines and the ultimate retaliations by the other side. An unfortunate side effect took place in 1987 when a United States Navy frigate, the USS Stark, on patrol in the Persian Gulf to protect the oil lifeline to the Western world, was attacked and seriously damaged by a missile launched from an Iraqi warplane. A similar peripheral incident, again brought about by nervous trigger fingers, occurred in early 1988 when the U.S. cruiser, USS Vincennes, escorting merchant shipping through the Gulf, mistakenly shot down an Iranian commercial airliner with a fearful loss of life.

Within weeks of that tragedy, the last barrier to a negotiated settlement was overcome when Iran formally accepted the UN's proposal for a cease-fire to be followed by peace talks. The United Nations Iran-Iraq Military Observer Group (UNIIMOG) arose from those efforts in August 1988 and military inspection teams were soon in-country to monitor the cease-fire and supervise the withdrawal of all forces. Patrolling from vehicles, helicopters, mule-back and even skis, owing to the treacherous terrain, the UN observers averaged 64 separate scouting trips per day to investigate actual or alleged breaches of the truce provisions. The UNIIMOG activities ended in 1991 without a total resolution of all of the UN's goals. Although minor incidents have occurred since that time, Iraq's involvement in the Gulf War seems to have diverted their attentions elsewhere.

14. UNGOMAP - United Nations Good Offices Mission in Afghanistan and Pakistan

MANDATE: To assist the Representative of the Secretary-General to lend his good offices to the parties in ensuring the implementation of the Agreements on the Settlement of the Situation Relating to Afghanistan and, in this context, to investigate and report possible violations of any of the provisions of the Agreements.

BACKGROUND: In December 1979, the forces of the Soviet Union entered Afghanistan in response to a reported request for assistance from the Afghanistan Government against the insurgent movements in the country. More than 100,000 Soviet troops were eventually deployed and they soon became embroiled in a long and costly conflict with the mujahideen, the Afghanistan resistance. The United Nations General Assembly, in a special session, strongly deplored the armed intervention and called for "the immediate, unconditional and total withdrawal of the foreign troops from Afghanistan". However, in the first phases of the armed intervention, no acceptable response was forthcoming from the Soviet Union which stood firm on its claim that it had reacted to what was deemed a legitimate request for assistance from a friendly, neighboring government. It also became evident, though formal proof could never be established, that Pakistan, which shared a long border with Afghanistan, was the conduit for supplying the mujahideen rebels with large quantities of arms obtained through other foreign sources.

Over the course of the next six years, as the bloody internal conflict dragged on, the United Nations indirectly conducted a series of on-again, off-again negotiations with the warring factions, always in the hope that a spark of compromise could be fanned. Finally, in 1988, as Soviet casualties mounted to immense proportions and internal pressures within the USSR became unbearable, the Soviet Union bowed to the inevitable and agreed to a peace process which soon led to the Geneva Accords.

Country/Location	Afghanistan, Pakistan
Dates	May 1988 to March 1990
Countries Participating	(10) Austria, Canada, Denmark, Fiji, Finland, Ghana, Ireland, Nepal, Poland, Sweden
Maximum Srength	50 military observers (1988)
Current Strength	0
Fatalities	None
Medal Number	1, 11, 12 (depending on parent organization)
CLASP(S)	UNGOMAP, OSGAP

Formally known as the Agreements on the Settlement of the Situation Relating to Afghanistan, it called for four elements to wit: a bilateral agreement between Afghanistan and Pakistan on non-interference, a declaration by the U.S. and USSR on international guarantees, an agreement on the voluntary return of refugees and an agreement on settlement.

The function created to supervise the above accords was the United Nations Good Offices Mission in Afghanistan and Pakistan (UNGOMAP). Owing to the minimal size projected for this effort, no new personnel were to be drawn from the member nations. Rather, as in a number of previous UN activities, the three missions active at that time, UNTSO, UNDOF and UNIFIL provided the necessary manpower. Most of the individual facets of the four-part agreement were generally carried out at the prescribed times but the element dealing with repatriation of Afghan refugees was not fulfilled. The UNGOMAP mission, however, was terminated in 1990. An unofficial clasp, OSGAP, has been created to commemorate that follow-on effort.

15. UNAVEM I - United Nations Angola Verification Mission I

UNAVEM: The ribbon contains a central broad band of UN blue flanked by three equal stripes of black, white and red, with wide yellow bands at either end. The yellow, red and black are representative of the Angolan national flag, with the white representing the UN presence in the country.

Country/Location	Angola
Dates	January 1989 to May 1991
Countries Participating	(10) Algeria, Argentina, Brazil, Congo, Czechoslovakia, India, Jordan, Norway, Spain, Yugoslavia
Maximum Srength	70 military observers (1989)
Current Strength	0
Fatalities	None
Medal Number	15
CLASP(S)	None

MANDATE: To verify the redeployment of Cuban troops northwards and their phased and total withdrawal from the territory of Angola in accordance with the timetable agreed between Angola and Cuba.

BACKGROUND: The world-wide desire for independence which had commenced after World War II started slowly in Africa, the most colonized region on Earth, but by the second half of the 20th century the movement was in high gear. Most typical was the area of Angola in south-west Africa which had been under Portuguese control since 1583 and had been the center of a thriving slave trade until the middle 19th century. In 1961, however, a guerilla war broke out which, after 14 grueling and bloody years, had forced Portugal to grant total independence to Angola in 1975. As had been the case elsewhere, the Portuguese had not educated the native population, nor had they schooled them in the administrative skills necessary to efficiently and successfully run the country.

Three separate and politically diverse groups then attempted to fill the vacuum created by the Portuguese withdrawal. These were the National Front, based in neighboring Zaire, the Soviet-sponsored Popular Front for the Liberation of Angola (MPLA) and the National Union for the Total Independence of Angola (UNITA) which received strong backing from South Africa and the United States. The result was a bloody civil war which caused the deaths of thousands of natives, drove most of the remaining white population out of the country and left the former colony in a state of economic chaos. By the following year, with the assistance of armed forces from Cuba and strong economic backing from the Soviet Union, the MPLA had gained control of the major portion of the country and assumed most of the duties of government. However, fierce fighting was still raging between the various factions when the United Nations took up the question in late 1988.

By that time, with most of their strategic and political objectives having been accomplished, the Governments of Cuba and Angola agreed to a United States initiative to participate with South Africa in a conference which would lead to the total withdrawal of all foreign forces from Angola. The agreements, signed by all of the participants on 22 December 1988, called for Cuba to remove its troops from the region under the supervision of a new UN effort, the United Nations Angola Verification Mission (UNAVEM). Additionally, all the signatories agreed that their countries would not violate the territorial integrity of any other State in southwestern Africa. By 1 April 1989, the first phase of troop withdrawal took place and, over the next 27 months, most of the 50,000 Cuban troops in Angola were withdrawn. Although the evacuation process was marred by the inevitable sporadic attacks, the final removal of all forces was accomplished and UNAVEM was declared a success and officially terminated in June 1991. The United Nations created a follow up mission, United Nations Angola Verification Mission II, in 1991

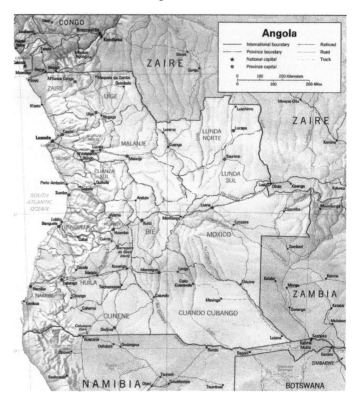

16. UNTAG - United Nations Transition Assistance Group in Namibia

UNTAG: The centre of the UNTAG ribbon contains five equal stripes in black, yellow, red, green and royal blue, the colours of the five Olympic Rings and representing the five continental regions of the world, all of which were represented in either the military or civilian police components of UNTAG. The centre is flanked by equal bars of a buff or sand colour to represent the Kalahari and Namib deserts with equal bands of UN blue appearing at each end.

Country/Location	Namibia, Angola
Dates	April 1989 to March 1990
Countries Participating	(50) Australia, Austria, Bangladesh, Barbados, Belgium, Canada, China, Congo, Costa Rica, Czechoslovakia, Denmark, Egypt, Federal Republic of Germany, Fiji, Finland, France, German Democratic Republic, Ghana, Greece, Guyana, Hungary, India, Indonesia, Ireland, Italy, Jamaica, Japan, Kenya, Malaysia, Netherlands, New Zealand, Nigeria, Norway, Pakistan, Panama, Peru, Poland, Portugal, Singapore, Spain, Sudan, Sweden, Switzerland, Thailand, Togo, Trinidad/Tobago, Tunisia, United Kingdom, USSR, Yugoslavia.
Maximum Srength	8,993 military observers (1989)
Current Strength	0
Fatalities	19
Medal Number	16
CLASP(S)	None

MANDATE: To assist the Special Representative of the Secretary-General to ensure the early independence of Namibia through free and fair elections under the supervision and control of the United Nations.

BACKGROUND: The details behind the independence of Namibia are quite unique in the history of southwestern Africa since they involved another United Nations peace-keeping mission in an adjoining country. Like most of the present nations on the African continent, Namibia also had its roots in the colonial movements of the late 19th and early 20th centuries. The region, then known as South-West Africa, came under the influence of the German Empire when a German company set up a small trading post in Lüderitz, a coastal town just on the edge of the Namib Desert. Germany annexed the territory in 1890 and declared it a protectorate, a status which it maintained until World War I when South African forces seized the country. It was mandated to South Africa by the League of Nations in 1920 and remained under Pretoria's control for over 45 years. A number of efforts were made by South Africa to annex the territory and make it their fifth province but world opinion and the World Court halted the undertaking.

In the interim, however, the United Nations had been pressuring the South African Government to renounce its mandate and place the country under UN control to speed the total independence of what is now known as Namibia. The South African Government, however, steadfastly refused to recognize the UN's authority and the status quo was maintained.

In 1966, however, the same independence fever that had swept through the colonial world since World War II erupted and the Marxist group known as the South-West Africa People's Organization (SWAPO) initiated a guerilla war to achieve independence. The results, as in previous instances of internal warfare abetted by outside influences (in this case, Cuba) were predictable and resulted in thousands of innocent civilian casualties.

The United Nations had attempted to mediate the dispute since the time of the original outbreaks but many bloody years and failed diplomatic efforts took place before the United States mediated a peace agreement between South Africa, Angola and Cuba. The agreement, based on a 1978 UN plan was signed in 1988 as part of the cease-fire in Angola. It provided for the removal of Cuban troops from the country and the holding of free general elections under the guidance and supervision of the newly-established United Nations Transition Assistance Group in Namibia (UNTAG). The elections provided a new president, a new constitution and a democratic government and UNTAG was terminated in 1990.

Royal Australian Engineers deploy. UN Photo.

17. ONUCA - United Nations Observer Group in Central America

ONUCA: The medal ribbon contains five narrow green stripes to represent the five countries involved. These five green stripes are separated by four equal white stripes. The central group is flanked by two equal bands of sea blue to represent the Pacific Ocean and the Caribbean Sea, flanked in turn by two broad bands of UN blue to represent the United Nations' presence in the area. Ninety days of service in the Mission are required to qualify for the medal.

Country/Location	Costa Rica, El Salvador, Guatemala, Honduras, Nicaragua
Dates	December 1989 to January 1992
Countries Participating	(11) Argentina, Brazil, Canada, Colombia, Ecuador, Federal Republic of Germany, India, Ireland, Spain, Sweden, Venezuela
Maximum Srength	1,098 military observers (1990)
Current Strength	0
Fatalities	None
Medal Number	17
CLASP(S)	None

MANDATE: To verify compliance by the Governments of Costa Rica, El Salvador, Guatemala, Honduras and Nicaragua with their undertakings to cease aid to irregular forces and insurrectionist movements in the region and not to allow their territory to be used for attacks in other States. In addition, ONUCA played a part in the voluntary demobilization of the Nicaraguan Resistance and monitored a cease-fire and the separation of forces agreed by the Nicaraguan parties as part of the demobilization process.

BACKGROUND: The countries of Central America, sometimes referred to as "Banana Republics" by other nations because the growing of tropical fruits is so widespread, have been hotbeds of political turmoil and civil wars for nearly one hundred years. In the words of one observer, "...the Governments seem to change as often as some people change their shoes." as power see-sawed back and forth between civilian rule and the inevitable military take-over. In the process, hundreds of thousands of lives were lost and countless numbers of people, both civilian and military, simply disappeared.

A Venezuelan soldier stands guard at camp where the Nicaraguan resistance surrender their weapons to ONUCA. UN Photo.

The task of trying to maintain peace in some of the poorest countries in the Western Hemisphere had been assumed by the United States under the aegis of the Monroe Doctrine during the early part of the 20th century, resulting in U.S. military intervention in Cuba, Haiti, the Dominican Republic and, as late as 1933, in Nicaragua. However, the world of the 1970s had changed drastically from the time that the U.S. could wield its "big stick" and dictate policy. The Communist take-over in Cuba in 1959 had added a brand-new player to the game of political intrigue as the Castro regime attempted to export their ideology to any vulnerable nation in the region. It was thus in 1988 when the Marxist Sandinista Government of Nicaraguan was actively assisting left-wing insurgent guerilla forces in the neighboring countries of Honduras and El Salvador. Nicaragua also had to deal with a civil war of its own as U.S.-supported anti-Sandinista Contras were carrying out guerrilla raids in an attempt to overturn the Cuban-backed Government of President Anastasio Somoza. In this atmosphere, the United States sent 3,200 troops into Honduras to maintain that nation's sovereignty after border violations by Nicaraguan troops.

Throughout all of the strife, other members of the Organization of American States (OAS), in particular Colombia, Mexico, Panama and Venezuela, had been striving to get the disputants to agree to a comprehensive regional peace place which they had drafted. It was not until 1989, however, that a summit conference involving the five Central American countries and the United Nations Secretary-General could be arranged. From this meeting came a new mission, the United Nations Observer Group in Central America (ONUCA) which employed military personnel to supervise the ensuing truce, the removal of foreign troops from all signatory nations and the demobilization of all troops. The conflicts in the region having been declared resolved, the ONUCA mission was terminated in January 1992.

18. UNIKOM - United Nations Iraq-Kuwait Observation Mission

UNIKOM: The broad buff-colored bands represent the wide expanse of desert in Iraq and Kuwait and the light blue center signifies the thin blue United Nations line in the sand.

Country/Location	Iraq, Kuwait
Dates	April 1991 to Oct 6, 2003
Countries Participating	(36) Argentina, Austria, Bangladesh, Canada, Chile, China, Denmark, Fiji, Finland, France, Germany, Ghana, Greece, Hungary, India, Indonesia, Ireland, Italy, Kenya, Malaysia, Nigeria, Norway, Pakistan, Poland, Romania, Russian Federation, Senegal, Singapore, Sweden, Switzerland, Thailand, Turkey, United Kingdom, United States, Uruguay, Venezuela
Maximum Srength	1,187 military observers
Current Strength	0
Fatalities	18 (2003)
Medal Number	18
CLASP(S)	None

MANDATE: Originally established as an unarmed observation mission with the mandate to monitor the Khawr 'Abd Allah waterway between Iraq and Kuwait and the Demilitarized Zone (DMZ), to deter violations of the boundary through its presence in and surveillance of the DMZ, and to observe any hostile action mounted from the territory of one State against the other. In 1993, following a series of incidents, the Security Council increased UNIKOM's strength and extended its terms of reference to include the capacity to take physical action to prevent violations of the DMZ and of the newly demarcated boundary between Iraq and Kuwait.

BACKGROUND: After the war between Iraq and Iran ended in 1988, Iraqi President Saddam Hussein turned his attention southward in an attempt to expand his influence in the Middle-East and the oil-producing nations in the area. After some preliminary sabre-rattling, Iraq launched a full-scale war on the neighboring Emirate of Kuwait on 2nd August 1990, completing the total occupation in a matter of a few days. Almost immediately, the United Nations Security Council met in an emergency session, condemning the unprovoked attack and demanding Iraq's immediate and unconditional withdrawal. Not only were the demands ignored, but Hussein defiantly declared Kuwait to be the 19th province of Iraq and mounted a massive campaign against the civilian population resulting in widespread atrocities and thousands of deaths. A few days later, the UN adopted a number of resolutions instituting harsh economic sanctions against Iraq and set 15 January 1991 as the deadline for Iraq's removal of all forces from Kuwait. In the meanwhile, on the assumption that Hussein would not be swayed, a confederation of countries representing the major oil producing and oil consuming nations of the world was created. The Coalition Forces, as the conglomerate was known, assembled the most massive collection of military might and sophisticated weaponry ever assembled. After the deadline had passed with

no response to the UN ultimatum, the Coalition launched a lightning, multifaceted air, sea and land attack on Iraqi forces in Kuwait and on Iraqi itself which, totally annihilated all resistance in a total of 100 hours.

In the meanwhile, the UN had set conditions and established the machinery for a cease-fire and its verification. That entity was a new mission, the United Nations Iraq-Kuwait Observation Mission (UNIKOM), which would monitor the ensuing events in Iraq and Kuwait. Iraq accepted the conditions for a cessation of hostilities and the cease-fire was formalized. In its initial stages, UNIKOM monitored the withdrawal of the Iraqi forces behind their own national borders and patrolled the DMZ established between the two frontiers. After a number of incidents on the DMZ involving Iraqi intrusion into Kuwait's territory, UNIKOM's force was strengthened so physical action could be taken to prevent small-scale intrusions into the neutral zone. The UNIKOM mission ended in 2003.

Five UNIKOM soldiers consulting a map in the Southern Sector of the demilitarized zone. The group includes (from left to right) one Fijian, one Chinese, two Russians and one Swede. UN Photo.

19. MINURSO - United Nations Mission for the Referendum in Western Sahara

MINURSO: The medal has a very wide central band of a sandy brown colour, representing the Sahara Desert, with two narrow bands of UN blue at either end. Ninety days of qualifying time is required for the award.

Country/Location	Western Sahara (Morocco)
Dates	September 1991 to present
Countries Participating	(36) Argentina, Australia, Austria, Bangladesh, Belgium, Canada, China, Egypt, El Salvador, Finland, France, Germany, Ghana, Greece, Guinea-Bissau, Honduras, Hungary, Ireland, Italy, Kenya, Korean Republic, Malaysia, Nigeria, Norway, Pakistan, Peru, Poland, Portugal, Russian Federation, Switzerland, Togo, Tunisia, United Kingdom, United States, Uruguay, Venezuela
Maximum Srength	3,000 authorized (1,700 military observers and troops, 300 police officers, approx. 1,000 civilian personnel)
Current Strength	465 (2020)
Fatalities	16 (2020)
Medal Number	19
CLASP(S)	None

MANDATE: Established in accordance with "the settlement proposals" as accepted by Morocco and the Frente Popular para la Liberación de Saguia el-Hamra y de Río de Oro (Frente POLISARIO) on 30 August 1988, to monitor a cease-fire, verify the reduction of Moroccan troops in the Territory, monitor the confinement of Moroccan and Frente POLISARIO troops to designated locations, ensure the release of all Western Saharan political prisoners or detainees, oversee the exchange of prisoners of war, implement the repatriation programme, identify and register qualified voters, organize and ensure a free referendum and proclaim the results. Of late, however, the Mission is limited to verifying the cease-fire and cessation of hostilities.

BACKGROUND: The small country of Morocco on the north-west corner of the African continent has a long history of involvement in the colonial period of the 19th and early 20th centuries during which time both France and Spain ruled portions of the region. Eleven years after the end of the Second World War, Morocco received its independence from France and expanded its territory to include the port of Tangier in 1956 and the former Spanish enclave of Ifni in 1969. In 1976, when Spain made the decision to give up most of her colonial possessions, she withdrew from her previously-held province of Spanish Sahara, directly adjacent to Morocco on the south-west. Within months, Morocco had stepped into the void and annexed some 70,000 square miles of the phosphate-rich territory which comprised the old areas of Río de Oro on the north and Saguia el-Hamra in the south. The remaining portion of Spanish Sahara was taken over by the bordering nation of Mauritania, also the recipient of independence from France.

Shortly thereafter, a new popular front, Frente POLISARIO, with major support from Algeria, proclaimed the region's independence and launched a bloody guerrilla war against the two occupying nations. When Mauritania signed a peace treaty with the insurgents in 1980, she relinquished all claims to Spanish Sahara but the Moroccan government soon seized and occupied the abandoned area. After years of bitter conflict, Moroccan forces held firm control of all major urban areas but the POLISARIO rebels operated at will in the sparsely-populated desert regions.

In 1985, the United Nations initiated a good offices mission to search for solutions to the fighting in the area now referred to as "Western Sahara". However, it was not until 1988 that an acceptable settlement plan could be placed before the warring sides and, in 1991, a new mission, the United Nations Mission for the Referendum in Western Sahara (MINURSO) was implemented. To date, the actual referendum date is still in dispute between the parties and the function of United Nations observers is limited to monitoring the cease-fire.

The settlement plan, as approved by the Security Council, provided for a transitional period for the preparation of a referendum in which the people of Western Sahara would choose between independence and integration with Morocco. The Special Representative of the Secretary-General was to have sole and exclusive responsibility over matters relating to the referendum and was to be assisted in his tasks by an integrated group of civilian, military and civilian police personnel, to be known as the United Nations Mission for the Referendum in Western Sahara.

On 29 April 2016, the Security Council adopted resolution 2285, calling upon the parties to the conflict to continue to show political will in order to enter into a more intensive and substantive phase of negotiations.

20. UNAVEM II - United Nations Angola Verification Mission II

UNAVEM II: The light blue and white areas represent the United Nations' presence in Angola and the yellow, red and black colors are those of the Angolan flag. .   This is the same ribbon as the original mission, UNAVEM I.

Country/Location	Angola
Dates	June 1991 to February 1995
Countries Participating	(25) Algeria, Argentina, Brazil, Canada, Colombia, Congo, Egypt, Guinea-Bissau, Hungary, India, Ireland, Jordan, Malaysia, Morocco, Netherlands, New Zealand, Nigeria, Norway, Senegal, Singapore, Slovakia, Spain, Sweden, Yugoslavia, Zimbabwe
Maximum Srength	1114 authorized (350 military observers, 126 police monitors, 83 international civilian staff, 155 local staff and 400 electoral observers)
Current Strength	0
Fatalities	5
Medal Number	20
CLASP(S)	None

MANDATE: Established to verify the arrangements agreed by the Angolan parties for the monitoring of the cease-fire and for the monitoring of the Angolan police during the cease-fire period and to observe and verify the elections in that country in accordance with the Peace Accords signed by the Angolan Government and the União Nacional para a Independência Total de Angola (UNITA).   Subsequent to the elections of 29 and 30 September 1992, verified by the United Nations as having been generally free and fair, the force continued its presence in Angola in order to help the two sides reach agreement on modalities for completing the peace process and, at the same time, to broker and help implement cease-fires at the national or local level.

BACKGROUND: The democratic concept of accepting the results of a national election until the next time its citizens go to the polls is so ingrained in the modern world that it becomes almost second-nature.   Even in countries which change governments often, the electorate is usually confident and patient enough to bide its time before ridding their country of an unworthy Head-of-State (or Parliament, Congress, etc.).   Unfortunately, this has not been the case in some countries which have achieved their independence only recently and do not have the history, traditions nor formal education to appreciate the concept.   This was the situation facing the United Nations after the cessation of hostilities and removal of all foreign forces from Angola in 1991.

With the approval of all parties, the UNAVEM mission (now designated, UNAVEM II) remained to supervise and monitor the various aspects of the cease-fire agreements and to observe and verify (not to organize) the national elections scheduled for September 1992. The balloting itself was peacefully completed on schedule despite some organizational and logistical difficulties. The results showed that more than 92 percent of Angola's 5.3 million citizens had voted and that the Movimento Popular para

a Libertaçao de Angola (MPLA) had won with 54 percent of the votes cast vs. 34 percent for UNITA, the party in power at the time of the civil war.

UNITA, however, denounced the results, claiming that the elections had been rigged through systematic and widespread manipulation and fraud.   At the same time, UNITA embarked on another civil war which raged all through 1992 and 1993.   By early 1994, UNITA forces held most of the countryside but the loss of life amongst civilians, mostly from starvation, was staggering. During this period, UNAVEM II's personnel could only observe and report on the steady disintegration of the countryside and the country's infrastructure.   However, after concerted efforts by the UN Security Council, a National Reconciliation Plan (the so-called Lusaka Protocol) was formulated and the parties were finally brought together. The resulting cease-fire generally held firm.   Large relief efforts were initiated and UNAVEM II was declared complete in February 1995.

Field Site in Sumbe Town, Angola. UN Photo.

21. ONUSAL - United Nations Observer Mission in El Salvador

ONUSAL: A medal was established in January 1992 for which 90 days of service is required for qualification. The medal has five equal bars, the centre being white, flanked by dark blue, and, at either end, by UN blue. The dark blue and white represent the national flag of El Salvador.

Country/Location	El Salvador
Dates	July 1991 to April 1995
Countries Participating	(17) Argentina, Austria, Brazil, Canada, Chile, Colombia, Ecuador, France, Guyana, India, Ireland, Italy, Mexico, Norway, Spain, Sweden, Venezuela
Maximum Srength	829 (683 military observers and police personnel plus 146 international civilian staff) (1992)
Current Strength	0
Fatalities	5
Medal Number	21
CLASP(S)	None

MANDATE: To verify the implementation of all agreements negotiated between the Government of El Salvador and the Frente Farabundo Martí para la Liberación Nacional (FMLN). The agreements involve a cease-fire and related measures, reform and reduction of the armed forces, creation of a new police force, reform of the judicial and electoral systems, human rights, land tenure and other economic and social issues. Subsequent to the cessation of the armed conflict between the Government of El Salvador and the FMLN on 15 December 1992, ONUSAL continued to monitor the remaining provisions of the peace agreements as well as verify the March 1994 elections in El Salvador.

BACKGROUND: In stark contrast with other Central American nations, El Salvador was able to maintain peaceful relations with her neighbors for the better part of 150 years since achieving her independence from Spain in 1821. This idyllic scenario changed drastically in the late 1970s when outside influences, particularly Cuba and Nicaragua, began to threaten El Salvador's sovereignty. In 1979, fearful of the government's lack of positive action against these elements. a military uprising took place which overthrew the government of President Carlos Humberto Romero. However, the new military-civilian junta could not successfully put down left-wing revolutionary forces which were receiving arms from Nicaragua and Cuba and the fierce civil war raged on. As passions rose, the rule of reason seemed to fall at a proportional rate and, before long, extreme right-wing death squads were roaming the country executing anyone suspected of even the slightest leftist sympathies. It has been estimated that nearly 100,000 people lost their lives during the 12 years of strife.

Like all such terrible conflicts of the past, it became obvious by 1989 that neither side could ever gain firm control of the country and unilaterally end the civil war. As a result of a complex negotiating process initiated by the two warring factions and conducted under the auspices of the United Nations, talks were initiated which endeavored to resolve the prolonged armed conflict, promote democratization of the country, guarantee human rights and reunify the Salvadorian society. The final agreements called for the establishment of a United Nations verification mission designated the United Nations Observer Mission in El Salvador (ONUSAL) and, after some additional maneuvering, it came into existence in July 1991.

The structure of the ONUSAL mission was unusual in that it contained individual branches to deal with each facet of the mandate, to wit: Political, Human Rights, Military and, subsequently, Elections. The war was not over by any means at that point but the parties finally signed the peace agreement and the incredibly costly war came to an end in January 1992. The ONUSAL mandate was later extended to permit UN teams to supervise the general elections which took place in March and April 1994 with few incidents. Since the major portions of the mandate were fulfilled and the fighting had halted, the ONUSAL mission was declared over in April 1995.

ONUSAL police from Mexico (second from left) and Spain (second from right) observing a Salvadoran police officer (far right) making a traffic stop. UN Observers provided training for El Salvador's national police force. UN Photo.

22. UNAMIC - United Nations Advance Mission in Cambodia

UNAMIC The light blue and white colors represent the flag of the United Nations while the red, gold and dark blue stripes signify the flags and coats-of-arms of the Kingdom of Cambodia and the Khmer Republic.

Country/Location	Cambodia
Dates	November 1991 to March 1992
Countries Participating	(24) Algeria, Argentina, Australia, Austria, Belgium, Canada, China, France, Germany, Ghana, India, Indonesia, Ireland, Malaysia, New Zealand, Pakistan, Poland, Russian Federation, Senegal, Thailand, Tunisia, United Kingdom, United States, Uruguay
Maximum Srength	1,090 military and civilian personnel (1992)
Current Strength	0
Fatalities	None
Medal Number	22
CLASP(S)	None

MANDATE: Originally, to assist the four Cambodian parties to maintain their cease-fire during the period prior to UNTAC's establishment and deployment and to initiate mine-awareness training of civilian populations. Later, the mandate was enlarged to include a major training program for Cambodians in mine-detection and mine-clearance and the mine-clearing of repatriation routes, reception centres and resettlement areas.

BACKGROUND: The recent history of the ancient kingdom of Cambodia is one replete with the struggle for independence from a colonial past, constant internal battles for power and continual efforts to resist attacks on her sovereignty from neighboring nations. During the conflicts which raged in the adjoining State of Vietnam during the twenty year period after Cambodia achieved total independence in 1953, her ruler, King Sihanouk, tried to maintain strict neutrality. However, as the War in Vietnam wore down, Vietnamese communists were reported to be providing arms and support to the Cambodian insurgent force, the Khmer Rouge. After a palace revolt in 1970 during which Premier Lon Nol seized power, the monarchy was abolished and a major civil war broke out between government forces and those of the Khmer Rouge. When the rebels captured the capital city of Phnom Penh in 1975, a new government was formed which was to bring chaos and ruin to the country.

Edicts were issued which forced the evacuation of all cities and towns and sent the country's entire population into the wilderness to clear the forests and jungles. More than one million people died from starvation or brutal executions during this period.

Relations with neighboring Vietnam also reached a new low in 1978 when fighting broke out along the border and escalated into a full-scale Vietnamese invasion. Once again, Phnom Penh fell to an invading force and years of severe hardship befell the Cambodians once again, this time at the hands of the Vietnamese.

However, the same Khmer Rouge insurgents who were once backed by Vietnam, continued to fight a savage guerrilla war against the invaders and the bloodshed continued well into the next decade.

After so many years of fighting, however, the Vietnamese invasion had cost that country dearly in both financial and human terms and Vietnam withdrew her troops from Cambodian soil in September 1989. In the void that followed, four separate groups vied for power but little was accomplished in creating a new central government. United Nations assistance was sought and provided in the form of two distinct missions with a single objective, to restore a semblance of normal existence to Cambodia. The first of these, the relatively small United Nations Advance Mission in Cambodia (UNAMIC) became operational immediately after the Paris agreements were signed by the four parties in 1991. UNAMIC functioned to pave the way for the second mission, UNTAC, described later in this text, by providing for the clearance of the thousands of mines laid during the civil strife. The mission was absorbed into UNTAC in March 1992.

23. UNPROFOR - United Nations Protection Force

UNPROFOR The basic color of the ribbon is light blue with a central band of red, flanked by white, representing the United Nations Protected Areas. On the left, the stripe of green represents the forests of Yugoslavia and an equal-sized band of brown on the right side epresents the mountains.

Country/Location	Former Yugoslavia (Bosnia, Herzegovina, Croatia, Serbia, Montenegro, Macedonia)
Dates	March 1992 to December 1995
Countries Participating	(43) Argentina, Australia, Bangladesh, Belgium, Brazil, Canada, Colombia, Czech Republic, Denmark, Egypt, Finland, France, Germany, Ghana, India, Indonesia, Ireland, Jordan, Kenya, Lithuania, Luxembourg, Malaysia, Nepal, Netherlands, New Zealand, Nigeria, Norway, Pakistan, Poland, Portugal, Russian Federation, Senegal, Slovakia, Spain, Sweden, Switzerland, Thailand, Tunisia, Turkey, Ukraine, United Kingdom, United States, Venezuela
Maximum Srength	39,922 (38,614 troops and support personnel, 637 military observers, 671 civilian police and 4,058 staff (1994)
Current Strength	0
Fatalities	207
Medal Number	23
CLASP(S)	None

Above photograph - UNPROFOR - Ambulances of the British contingent of UNPROFOR moving through the streets of Vukovar, which was destroyed by Serbian shelling. UN Photo

MANDATE: Croatia. Established in March 1992 as an interim arrangement to create the conditions of peace and security required for the negotiation of an overall settlement of the Yugoslav crisis. UNPROFOR's mandate was to ensure that the UN Protected Areas (UNPAs) are demilitarized, through the withdrawal or disbandment of all armed forces in them, and that all persons residing in them are protected from fear of armed attack. Later expanded to control the entry of civilians into the UNPAs and to perform immigration and customs functions at UNPA borders and international frontiers. Also extended to include monitoring of the demilitarization of the Prevlaka Peninsula near Dubrovnik and to ensure control of the Peruca Dam.

Bosnia & Herzegovina: Established in June 1992, after the deterioration of the situation in the area, to ensure the security and functioning of the airport in Sarajevo, the capital of Bosnia & Herzegovina, and the delivery of humanitarian assistance to Sarajevo and its environs was further expanded to support humanitarian relief throughout the region and to protect convoys of released civilian detainees. The mission also monitored compliance with the ban on all military flights in the airspace of Bosnia & Herzegovina. Macedonia: In December 1992, UNPROFOR was further deployed in the Former Yugoslav Republic of Macedonia to monitor and report any developments in its border areas which could undermine confidence and stability in that Republic and threaten its stability.

BACKGROUND: The sudden fall of Communism late in the 1980s produced a world-wide rebirth of democratic freedom in former Iron Curtain countries but also produced a totally unexpected fallout. Nations that contained widespread multinational and multiracial populations, apparently living together in harmony for many decades, started coming apart at the seams. The hatreds and suspicions, apparently held in check by the previous authoritarian socialist governments, suddenly surfaced in such areas as the USSR, Czechoslovakia, Romania and, of prime importance, Yugoslavia.

Here was the classic case of enmities, rivalries and religious differences, some dating back hundreds of years, that set neighbor against neighbor and destroyed the fabric of the country. With the death of President Tito in 1980, once-secret separatist groups in Croatia and Slovenia emerged and agitated for independence, leading to bloody confrontations and incredible destruction of property and the basic infrastructure. Starting in 1991, the United Nations attempted mediate the disputes and restore peace but with very little success. The United Nations Protection Force (UNPROFOR) mission was established in March 1992 to monitor the six portions of the former Yugoslavia but the task was a daunting one as the fighting continued with almost no letup, cease-fires were established and ignored and atrocities were reported on all sides. As the fighting spread, the UN's duties became more complex and the mission was terminated in 1995, being replaced by the UNCRO and UNPREDEP missions.

UNPROFOR - British contingent of UNPROFOR patrol poviding safety for civilians.   *UN Photo*

24. UNTAC - United Nations Transitional Authority in Cambodia

UNTAC The green background of the ribbon represents the paddies which cover most of Cambodia, the red and dark blue are major components of the Cambodian flag while the light blue and white are the colors of the United Nations flag.

Country/Location	Cambodia
Dates	Mar. 1992 to Sept. 1993
Countries Participating	(46) Algeria, Argentina, Australia, Austria, Bangladesh, Belgium, Brunei, Bulgaria, Cameroon, Canada, Chile, China, Colombia, Egypt, Fiji, France, Germany, Ghana, Hungary, India, Indonesia, Ireland, Italy, Japan, Jordan, Kenya, Malaysia, Morocco, Namibia, Nepal, Netherlands, New Zealand, Nigeria, Norway, Pakistan, Philippines, Poland, Russian Federation, Senegal, Singapore, Sweden, Thailand, Tunisia, United Kingdom, United States, Uruguay
Maximum Srength	19,350 military and civilian personnel (1993)
Current Strength	0
Fatalities	78
Medal Number	24
CLASP(S)	UNAMIC (later withdrawn)

MANDATE: Under the Agreement on a Comprehensive Settlement of the Cambodia Conflict, signed in Paris on 23 October 1991, the Supreme National Council of Cambodia (the SNC) is "the unique legitimate body and source of authority in which, throughout the transitional period, the sovereignty, independence and unity of Cambodia are enshrined". The SNC, which was made up of the four Cambodian factions, had delegated to the United Nations "all powers necessary" to ensure the implementation of the Agreement. UNTAC's mandate includes aspects relating to human rights, the organization and conduct of free and fair general elections, military arrangements, civil administration, the maintainance of law and order, the repatriation and resettlement of the Cambodian refugees and displaced persons and the rehabilitation of essential Cambodian infrastructure during the transitional period. The transitional period commenced with the entry into force of the Agreement (23 October 1991) and will terminate when the constituent assembly elected in conformity with the Agreement has approved the new Cambodian Constitution and transformed itself into a legislative assembly, and thereafter a new Cambodian Government has been created.

BACKGROUND: As previously discussed under the UNAMIC operation, a cease-fire and mine-clearance had been successfully achieved, the second phase, the United Nations Transitional Authority in Cambodia (UNTAC) prepared to take up its duties in that war-torn

country. Upon becoming operational on 15 March 1992, UNTAC absorbed all of the duties and personnel of UNAMIC under its own jurisdiction. Of prime importance was agreement amongst the four political factions, the Front Uni National pour un Cambodge Indépendent, Neutre, Pácifique et Coopératif (FUNCINPEC), the Khmer People's National Liberation Front (KPNLF), the Party of Democratic Kampuchea (PDK) and State of Cambodia (SOC) on the best way to achieve the goal of free elections agreed to in the Paris Agreement as well as the remainder of the mandated purposes.

Of the four groups, three fully cooperated with the UNTAC personnel but the fourth, the PDK (the former Khmer Rouge) refused to conform with the Paris Agreements. After the fact, PDK representatives reinterpreted some provisions of the treaty and refused to allow UNTAC forces to proceed with their deployment in areas under PDK control and did not provide necessary data on numbers of troops and matériel. After months of fruitless negotiations and a spate of violence in PDK-controlled areas, the UN decided to move ahead with the first step of the electoral process, voter registration and other aspects of military, civil, police, repatriation and rehabilitation efforts. The elections were held in May 1993 without the PDK and resulted in the division of power between the two major factions, FUNCINPEC and KPNLF. UNTAC forces withdrew as planned in September 1993 in spite of PDK agitation.

UNTAC peace-keepers from Bangladesh teach a Cambodian soldier to deactivate mines. Cambodia, 1992 UN Photo.

25. UNOSOM I - United Nations Operation in Somalia I

UNOSOM I The buff/sand background of the ribbon symbolizes the desert with a wide center band of United Nations blue flanked by narrow stripes of dark green representing hope.

Country/Location	Somalia
Dates	April 1992 to April 1993
Countries Participating	(16) Australia, Austria, Bangladesh, Belgium, Canada, Czechoslovakia, Egypt, Fiji, Finland, Indonesia, Jordan, Morocco, New Zealand, Norway, Pakistan, Zimbabwe
Maximum Srength	4,469 authorized (50 military observers, 3,500 security personnel, 719 logistic support personnel and 200 international civilian staff) (1992)
Current Strength	0
Fatalities	8
Medal Number	25
CLASP(S)	None

MANDATE: To monitor the cease-fire in Mogadishu, the capital of Somalia and to provide protection and security for United Nations personnel, equipment and supplies at the seaports and airports in Mogadishu and escort deliveries of humanitarian supplies from there to distribution centers in the city and its immediate environs. In August 1992, UNOSOM's mandate and strength were enlarged to enable it to protect the humanitarian convoys and distribution centers throughout Somalia.

BACKGROUND: The country of Somalia, lying on the eastern "horn" of Africa between the Gulf of Aden and the Indian Ocean, is another product of the failed policies of its previous colonial rulers. Formed from a union of British and Italian Somaliland, the country was ill-prepared for the responsibilities of independence owing to the generally poor level of public education, civil administration and the economy. An internal coup and a protracted war with neighboring Ethiopia, ending in 1988, did little to achieve any measure of political or economic stability in the region. In 1991, the twenty-one year rule of General Muhammad Siad Barre ended with an internal power struggle and the eruption of fierce tribal clashes within the country. The fighting between the rival bands led to some 300,000 casualties and, by mid-1992, an estimated 4.5 million people, over half the estimated population, were in danger of starvation owing to the civil war, drought and tribal conflicts. As early as March 1991, the United Nations had been heavily involved in humanitarian efforts to bring relief to the country

A UNOSOM radio expert installs radio equipment into a Pakistan Battalion jeep for deployment to field operations. UN Photo.

but the political chaos, deteriorating security situation, widespread banditry, looting and damage to the infrastructure compounded the problem and made the delivery of humanitarian supplies a logistical nightmare.

The deteriorating and appalling situation in Somalia led to concerted negotiations by the United Nations to mediate a peace settlement and, after many months of futile efforts, Letters of Agreement implementing a cease-fire were signed among the various factions. Among the provisions was the establishment of a new mission, the United Nations Operation in Somalia (UNOSOM), charged with the responsibility of monitoring the cease-fire and administering subsequent humanitarian efforts, recovery programs and institution-building. Once deployed in Mogadishu, they began the daunting task of bringing massive humanitarian assistance to the countryside. With the onset of such efforts, however, a period of looting by heavily armed gangs at the delivery and distribution points as well as docked ships and airfields took place, thus preventing the transport of humanitarian assistance to the country at large.

As a result, UNOSOM's mandate was enlarged to include an armed Unified Task Force (UNITAF) to provide protection and support for these efforts. Composed mainly of United States troops, the food shipments were stepped up but at the cost of significant casualties amongst the U.S. forces. In April 1993, the UNOSOM effort officially ended but all efforts continued as part of a follow-on mission designated UNOSOM II.

26. ONUMOZ - United Nations Operation in Mozambique

ONUMOZ The central, wide band of United Nations blue is flanked by narrow bands of white representing peace. The bands of green on each edge symbolize the tropical climate of Mozambique.

Country/Location	Mozambique
Dates	1992 to December 1994
Countries Participating	(40) Argentina, Australia, Austria, Bangladesh, Bolivia, Botswana, Brazil, Canada, Cape Verde, China, Czech Republic, Egypt, Finland, Ghana, Guinea-Bissau, Guyana, Hungary, India, Indonesia, Ireland, Italy, Japan, Jordan, Malaysia, Nepal, Netherlands, New Zealand, Nigeria, Norway, Pakistan, Portugal, Russian Federation, Spain, Sri Lanka, Sweden, Switzerland, Togo, United States, Uruguay, Zambia
Maximum Srength	6,576 military and 1,087 civilian personnel (1993)
Current Strength	0
Fatalities	24
Medal Number	26
CLASP(S)	None

Mozambicans wait to vote during UN-assisted Oct. 1994 elections. UN Photo.

MANDATE: In accordance with the General Peace Agreement, signed on 4 October 1992 in Rome by the President of the Republic of Mozambique and the President of the Resistência Nacional Moçambicana (RENAMO), the mandate of ONUMOZ included four elements as follows:

Political: To facilitate impartially the implementation of the Agreement, in particular by chairing the Supervisory and Monitoring Commission and its subordinate commissions.

Military: To monitor and verify the cease-fire, the separation and concentration of forces, their demobilization and the collection, storage and destruction of weapons; to monitor and verify the complete withdrawal of foreign forces and to provide security in the transport corridors; to monitor and verify the disbanding of private and irregular armed groups; to authorize security arrangements for vital infrastructures and to provide security for United Nations and other international activities in support of the peace process.

Electoral: To provide technical assistance and monitor the entire electoral process.

Humanitarian: To coordinate and monitor humanitarian assistance operations, in particular those relating to refugees, internally displaced persons, demobilized military personnel and the affected local population.

BACKGROUND: Mozambique, a nearly 300,000 square mile area on eastern Africa, was under the control of Portugal since the early 16th century but, like almost all of the colonial possessions in Africa after World War II, received its total independence in 1975 after ten years of struggle against the mother country. A new government was formed which moved the country towards the communist philosophy but an unstable economy caused by white emigration and a huge external national debt caused enormous problems. By the 1980s, a prolonged civil war and severe drought had brought on widespread famine and a resulting heavy loss of life. Even after the government repudiated the Marxist-Leninist philosophy and adopted a new constitution in 1989, internal unrest was still rampant.

At about this time, the United Nations became involved in attempts to mediate the dispute and on 4 October 1992, after 14 years of devastating civil war, the representatives of the government and RENAMO signed a General Peace Agreement in Rome. Under the agreements, a cease-fire was to be followed by separation of forces and demobilization, all under the direct supervision of the new mission, the United Nations Operation in Mozambique (ONUMOZ). Although the implementation of the entire UN mandate seemed painfully slow at times, by October 1994, most of the aims of the General Peace Agreement were in motion. Also of major importance at that time were the ongoing preparations for the general elections. Although the head of RENAMO expressed some reservations over the electoral process, the elections were declared free and fair. As the new government took office, the aims of ONUMOZ were declared completed and the mission was withdrawn in December 1994.

27. UNOSOM II - United Nations Operation in Somalia II

UNOSOM II The buff/sand background of the ribbon symbolizes the desert with a wide center band of United Nations blue flanked by narrow stripes of dark green representing hope. This is the same ribbon as for the original mission, UNOSOM I.

Country/Location	Somalia
Dates	May 1993 to March 1995
Countries Participating	(34) Australia, Bangladesh, Belgium, Botswana, Canada, Egypt, France, Germany, Ghana, Greece, India, Indonesia, Ireland, Italy, Korean Republic, Kuwait, Malaysia, Morocco, Nepal, Netherlands, New Zealand, Nigeria, Norway, Pakistan, Philippines, Romania, Saudi Arabia, Sweden, Tunisia, Turkey, United Arab Emirates, United States, Zambia, Zimbabwe
Maximum Strength	30,800 authorized (28,000 military personnel and approximately 2,800 civilian staff)
Current Strength	0
Fatalities	147
Medal Number	27
CLASP(S)	None

MANDATE: In March 1993, the United Nations Security Council, in response to the continuing degradation of the situation in Somalia, approved the Secretary-General's proposal for the second part of the United Nations Operation in Somalia (UNOSOM II) to take over from UNITAF and to expand the size and the mandate of UNOSOM II. The transfer of budgetary and administrative control as well as military command from UNITAF to UNOSOM II took place in May 1993. The mandate of UNOSOM II was to take appropriate action, including enforcement measures, to establish throughout Somalia a secure environment for humanitarian assistance. The mandate was to complete, through disarmament and reconciliation, the task begun by UNITAF for the restoration of peace, stability, law and order. UNOSOM II was also entrusted with assisting the Somali people in rebuilding their economy and social and political life, re-establishing the country's institutional structure, achieving national political reconciliation, recreating a Somali State based on democratic governance and rehabilitating the country's economy and infrastructure.

BACKGROUND: In March 1993, the presence of armed United Nations troops in-country seemed to have had a positive impact on the security situation in Somalia and on the effective delivery of humanitarian assistance. However, a secure environment had not yet been established, there was no effective functioning government in the country and no organized civilian police force nor effective national armed force had yet been created. Based on that assessment of the situation, the Secretary-General recommended that a transition from the Unified Task Force (UNITAF) to a larger, better-equipped body (UNOSOM II) be effected without delay. Once formally instituted, the first item on the agenda was the seemingly endless rash of violence that plagued all areas, both cities and countryside alike. Some clan leaders, fearful of losing power, resisted all efforts to disarm resulting in armed clashes and ambushes directed against UN troops. A series of swift counterattacks by UNOSOM II forces, however, did much to restore a small measure of order in a few affected areas, mostly in and around the capital city of Mogadishu, but casualties were heavy. All through 1994 and into 1995, UNOSOM II efforts were also directed to the humanitarian aspects contained in the mandate but, again, the lack of stability in the countryside made such efforts close to impossible. Since disarmament of all combatants was the prelude to accomplishing all the remaining elements of the mandate, concerted diplomatic activities were directed towards that goal but with few actual results. A series of conferences between the various factions resulted in statements repudiating the use of force as a means to resolve conflicts but the independently-minded clan chiefs continually broke the arranged truces. Although some progress was made in the areas of establishment of a national police force and humanitarian aid, the entire UNOSOM experience was proven an unfortunate failure. When UN troops withdrew in March 1995, no functioning government existed and, to this day, armed rebel factions still rule various portions of the country.

Secretary-General presents Peace Medal to former Force Commander of United Nations Operation in Somalia. UN Photo

28. UNOMUR - United Nations Observer Mission in Uganda and Rwanda

UNOMUR The central wide band of United Nations blue is flanked by narrow bands of white which signify peace. The equal-sized stripes of black, gold and red on each edge represent the colors of the Ugandan flag.

Country/Location	Uganda, Rwanda
Dates	June 1993 to September 1994
Countries Participating	(9) Bangladesh, Botswana, Brazil, Canada, Hungary, Netherlands, Senegal, Slovakia, Zimbabwe
Maximum Srength	105 authorized (81 military observers, 17 international staff and 7 locally-recruited personnel) (1994)
Current Strength	0
Fatalities	None
Medal Number	28
CLASP(S)	None

MANDATE: Established in 1993 to monitor the cease-fire established between the Government of Rwanda and the Rwandese Patriotic Front (RPF) and to assist the efforts of the Organization of African Unity (OAU) in finding a permanent political settlement of grievances that led to the civil war then raging in the country near the Uganda-Rwanda border. In addition, to deploy observers along the 150 kilometer common border to prevent the military use of the area, especially for the transport of military supplies. Later, the efforts were to be taken over by, and the manpower and resources absorbed into a follow-on mission, the United Nations Assistance Mission in Rwanda (UNAMIR).

BACKGROUND: The history and development of the African nation of Rwanda is another classic example of the short-sightedness of the once-dominant colonial powers in dealing with the native populations. Two native groups, the Hutus, representing 90% of the population, and the Tutsis, a proud warrior people, had struggled for power and control for centuries. With the advent of Belgian control after World War I, little was done to prepare either native segment for their ultimate transition to independence in 1962, resulting in a bloody civil war and the exile of the Tutsi tribe. Subsequent attempts to attain power by the Tutsis via invasion and civil strife led to further violence, massacres and atrocities. Finally, an accommodation seemed to have been reached and a democratic, multiparty government was established.

However, the peace was not long-lived as, in October 1990, fighting between government troops and the Tutsis, represented by the Rwandese Patriotic Front (RPF), broke out once again, this time across the border between Rwanda and its northern neighbor, Uganda. Despite a number of cease-fires brokered by the OAU, the ethnic strife continued sporadically but blew up into a full-fledged civil war in February 1993. At this point, United Nations assistance was urgently sought, which led to pledges by both sides to commit to a cease-fire and to a negotiated settlement. They also pledged to commit themselves to providing adequate security and protection for displaced persons. Finally, they consented to the establishment and deployment of a new force, the United Nations Observer Mission in Uganda-Rwanda (UNOMUR) to oversee and enforce the mandate.

The mission's advance party arrived in August 1993, paving the way for the entire force one month later. At the same time, ongoing talks between the parties took place in Arusha, Tanzania, widely expanding the desired United Nations involvement in Rwanda to include issues of disarmament, demobilization, humanitarian relief and the establishment of a broad-based government. To this end an expanded mission, UNAMIR, was proposed and UNOMUR's manpower and assets were officially absorbed into the new operation.

Former UN Commander visits civilians. UN Photo

29. UNOMIG - United Nations Observer Mission in Georgia

UNOMIG The center of the ribbon is United Nations blue, flanked on either side by white stripes representing the snow-covered mountain tops of the Caucasus, then green stripes for the coastal plains and foothills, edged in dark blue denoting the Black Sea.

Country/Location	Republic of Georgia
Dates	August 1993 to June 2009
Countries Participating	(23) Albania, Austria, Bangladesh, Cuba, Czech Republic, Denmark, Egypt, France, Germany, Greece, Hungary, Indonesia, Jordan, Korean Republic, Pakistan, Poland, Russian Federation, Sweden, Switzerland, Turkey, United Kingdom, United States, Uruguay
Maximum Srength	136 military observers (1994)
Current Strength	0
Fatalities	12 (All UN Personnel)
Medal Number	29
CLASP(S)	None

MANDATE: Established in August 1993 to verify compliance with the cease-fire agreement of 27 July 1993 with special attention to the situation in the City of Sukhumi; to investigate reports of cease-fire violations and to attempt to resolve such incidents with the parties involved; and to report to the Secretary-General on the implementation of its mandate including, in particular, violations of the cease-fire agreement. After July 1994, UNOMIG's mandate was expanded to (a) monitor and verify the implementation of the Agreement on a Cease-Fire and Separation of Forces, (b) to observe the operation of the Commonwealth of Independent States (CIS or Russian Federation) peace-keeping force, (c) to verify that troops do not remain in or re-enter the security zone and that heavy military equipment does not remain or is not reintroduced in the security zone or the restricted weapons zone, (e) to monitor the storage areas for heavy military equipment withdrawn from the security zone and restricted weapons zone, (e) to monitor the withdrawal of Georgian troops from the Kodori Valley to places beyond the frontiers of Abkhazia, (f) to patrol regularly the Kodori Valley, (g) to investigate reported or alleged violations of the Agreement and attempt to resolve such incidents.

BACKGROUND: The country of Georgia, strategically located on the Black Sea, is another case of a long, enforced marriage to a mother country that broke apart at the seams under the pressures of extreme nationalism. A constituent part of Russia and the USSR since 1801, separatist feelings had smoldered for many years, with bloody, repressionist actions having been taken by the central government to quell such movements. However, with the dissolution of the Soviet Union in December 1991, Georgia became an independent state. In 1992, an uprising took place in Abkhazia, an autonomous region within Georgia, which was crushed by government forces. A cease-fire agreement ending the armed revolt was signed and inspection teams from both sides plus the Russian Federation were established. However, the pact was never fully implemented and both sides continually

violated the cease-fire. The situation steadily deteriorated and a new major crisis occurred in 1993 when the Abkhazis, allegedly supported by the Russians, launched a bloody military campaign against the central government. In the vicious ethnic war that ensued, the Abkhazis gained the upper hand and exercised total control over a good portion of the region.

The United Nations, in response to requests from all of the interested parties, became involved in the dispute and the United Nations Observer Mission in Georgia (UNOMIG) was formed and deployed. Breaches of the cease-fire and, more importantly, human rights violations were reported on both sides while additional peace talks and negotiations were taking place. In May 1994, the UN mandate was expanded, an additional cease-fire agreement was ratified and a CIS peace-keeping force was also deployed inside the war-ravaged region. With the return to a condition of relative calm, Georgia has since been accepted as a member of the CIS and the UNOMIG operation remained in place until June 2009 when the mandate was not extended by the Security Council.

Korean Paratrooper greets local children.UN Photo

30. UNOMIL - United Nations Observer Mission in Liberia

UNOMIL The central wide band of United Nations blue flanked by narrow bands of white signify the peace. On the left, a stripe of deep blue represents the Atlantic Ocean littoral, reliefs, heights and rains. The red stripe on the right edge denotes the sacrifice of human blood in the carnage.

Country/Location	Liberia
Dates	1993 to Sept 1997
Countries Participating	(21) Austria, Bangladesh, Belgium, Brazil, China, Congo, Czech Republic, Egypt, Guinea-Bissau, Hungary, India, Jordan, Kenya, Malaysia, Netherlands, Pakistan, Poland, Russian Federation, Slovakia, Sweden, Uruguay
Maximum Srength	374 (309 military observers and 65 military medical personnel)
Current Strength	0
Fatalities	None
Medal Number	30
CLASP(S)	None

MANDATE: Established in 1993 to support the efforts of the already-existing Economic Community of West African States (ECOWAS) in the implementation of the Cotonou Peace Agreement, including:

Military: To monitor the cease-fire to take effect on 1 August 1993 and report on the steps taken towards the encampment, disarmament and demobilization of military units.

Political: To monitor the establishment of a single Liberian National Transitional Government having three branches: legislative, executive and judicial. Also to oversee the preparations for, and the execution of general and presidential elections to take place within 7 months of the signing of the Agreement and set out the modalities for the elections to be supervised by a reconstituted Electoral Commission.

Humanitarian: To facilitate the delivery of humanitarian assistance throughout Liberia using the most direct routes and under inspection to ensure compliance with the embargo provisions of the Agreement; to facilitate the speedy return of refugees and their reintegration into their communities.

BACKGROUND: The small nation of Liberia on the west coast of Africa is, from a political standpoint, the most unique country on the entire continent. Having been founded in 1822 as a home for former American slaves, it has never come under the control of any European country, even under the fierce political and economic rivalries of colonial expansionism. Moreover, it managed to maintain its neutrality and relatively peaceful existence until the 1980's when a series of civil uprisings and military coups seized power. Although there was a brief period of relative tranquility in the region, a major civil war broke out in December 1989 with rebel forces making major territorial gains and threatening the capital city of Monrovia. The war claimed the lives of nearly 150,000 civilians and drove nearly 700,000 more to

sanctuary in neighboring countries. By this time, Liberia was badly divided, with the Interim Government of National Unity (IGNU) administering Monrovia and its environs, the National Patriotic Front of Liberia (NPFL) controlling most of the country and the United Liberation Movement of Liberia for Democracy (ULIMO) having taken control of the remaining areas.

The ECOWAS states attempted to mediate the dispute but after many cease-fires failed to hold, the United Nations was asked to step-in and assist with its own peace-keeping efforts in 1993. Thus was the United Nations Observer Mission in Liberia (UNOMIL) formed in an area of the world once considered free of factional differences and tribal hatreds. Although another cease-fire agreement was reached, this time at a conference in Cotonou in neighboring Benin, it too suffered the same fate as previous peace agreements and severe factional warfare actually intensified rather than subsided. A new accord, reached in August 1995, called for the rival factions to share power but new and bloody fighting erupted in early 1996, leaving ECOWAS, UNOMIL and an enormous refugee population in a state of chaos.

However, a ceasefire was established and elections held in July 1997. This led to the establishment of a democratically elected government and effectively ended the war. UNOMIL 's principal objective was achieved and a post conflict peace building support office was designated as UNOL (UN Peace Building Support Office in Liberia).

31. UNAMIR - United Nations Assistance Mission for Rwanda

UNAMIR The central wide band of United Nations blue is flanked by narrow bands of white signifying the peace. The black color represents the volcanic lava and the world-famous gorillas. Green is the color of the local bush vegetation and red represents the Rwandan soil.

Country/Location	Rwanda
Dates	October 1993 to March 1996
Countries Participating	(40) Argentina, Australia, Austria, Bangladesh, Belgium, Brazil, Canada, Chad, Congo, Djibouti, Egypt, Ethiopia, Fiji, Germany, Ghana, Guinea, Guinea-Bissau, Guyana, India, Jordan, Kenya, Malawi, Mali, Netherlands, Niger, Nigeria, Pakistan, Poland, Romania, Russian Federation, Senegal, Slovakia, Spain, Switzerland, Togo, Tunisia, United Kingdom, Uruguay, Zambia, Zimbabwe
Maximum Srength	5,540 authorized (5,400 military personnel, 50 military police and 90 civilian police personnel) (1994)
Current Strength	0
Fatalities	26
Medal Number	31
CLASP(S)	None

MANDATE: Established in 1993 with the prime objective of contributing to the establishment and maintenance of a climate conducive to the secure installation and subsequent operation of the transitional Government of Rwanda. The mission was to assist in ensuring the security of the capital city of Kigali; monitor the cease-fire agreement including the establishment of an expanded demilitarized zone (DMZ) and demobilization procedures; monitor the security situation during the period leading up to national elections; assist with mine clearance; investigate alleged non-compliance with any provisions of the peace agreement and provide security for the repatriation of Rwandese refugees and displaced persons and assist in the coordination of humanitarian assistance activities in conjunction with relief operations.

BACKGROUND: When fighting broke out along the border between Uganda and Rwanda in 1993, the United Nations had deployed an observer force to attempt to obtain a political settlement of the civil war raging at the time and to station observers along the border as a deterrent to further violence (see UNOMUR, page 60). As the result of negotiations held in Arusha, Tanzania, concluded in August 1993, a comprehensive peace agreement was signed providing for the establishment of a democratically-elected transitional government. Additionally, the United Nations was requested to expand its present mandate to include those tasks necessary to insure the fairness of the upcoming elections. Recognizing the broad new scope of activities required, a second mission, the United Nations Assistance Mission for Rwanda

(UNAMIR) was conceived and the first contingent was deployed in October 1993.

Although the disputes were apparently settled at last, the auspicious beginning soon deteriorated into a quagmire of suspicion, factional hatreds and, ultimately, into brutal tribal warfare. The trigger seemed to have been an unfortunate plane crash at Kigali Airport in April 1994 which claimed the lives of all on-board including the Presidents of Rwanda and neighboring Burundi. Following this tragedy, wide-spread rumors concerning sabotage to the aircraft began to circulate within the country. When no full-fledged investigation was immediately launched into the cause of the accident, widespread killings, having both ethnic and political motivations, began in Kigali and spread to other portions of the country. A full-fledged civil war was soon in progress resulting in country-wide massacres of the Hutu opposition and intelligentsia, as well as members of the Tutsi minority and other supporters of the Rwandese Patriotic Front (RPF).

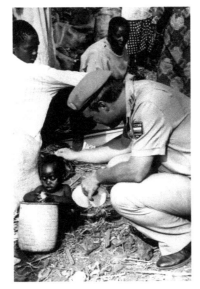

United Nations assistance Mission in Rwanda. A Russian UNAMIR soldier plays with a baby in a camp for Twandan refugees.

The mission lasted from October 1993 to March 1996. Its activities were meant to aid the peace process between the Hutu-dominated Rwandese government and the Tutsi-dominated rebel Rwandan Patriotic Front (RPF). The UNAMIR mission generally failed due to the limitations of its rules of engagement in preventing the Rwandan genocide and outbreak of fighting. The mission is thus regarded as a major failure.

32. UNMIH - United Nations Mission in Haiti

UNMIH The center of the ribbon is designed with the half blue-half red design of the flag of the Republic of Haiti and the white and light blue edge stripes denote friendship. UNSMIH, the follow-on mission in Haiti, uses the same ribbon with the clasp, UNSMIH.

Country/Location	Haiti
Dates	Sept 1993 to June 1996
Countries Participating	(34) Algeria, Antigua and Barbuda, Argentina, Austria, Bahamas, Bangladesh, Barbados, Belize, Benin, Canada, Djibouti, France, Guatemala, Guinea-Bissau, Guyana, Honduras, India, Ireland, Jamaica, Jordan, Mali. Nepal, Netherlands, New Zealand, Pakistan, Philippines, Russian Federation, St.Kitts & Nevis, St.Lucia, Suriname, Togo, Trinidad and Tobago, Tunisia, United States
Maximum Strength	6,065 military personnel and 847 civilian police (1995)
Current Strength	0
Fatalities	6
Medal Number	32
CLASP(S)	None

MANDATE: Established in 1993 to assist the Permanent Council of the Organization of American States (OAS) and its associated International Civilian Mission in Haiti (MICIVIH) in restoring the democratic institutional framework in Haiti with special attention to the observance of the rights to life, the integrity and security of the person, personal liberty, freedom of expression and freedom of association. The mandate also called for assistance in the modernization of the armed forces, establishment of a new police force, and technical assistance in the organization of free and fair elections.

BACKGROUND: Like many of her Caribbean neighbors, Haiti's history during the early 20th century bordered on the chaotic. Following one period of political violence in 1914, U.S. Marines were sent in to restore peace and occupied the country until 1934. After World War II, Haiti slipped into a family dictatorship which ended with the self-imposed exile of President Jean Claude Duvalier. Rather than improving, however, the nation fell further into disarray with no fewer than five governments over the next four years. With the democratic election of Father Jean-Bertrand Aristede in 1990, it was hoped that a measure of normalcy had returned to that island nation but a bloody uprising, led by the private militia of the Duvalier family and a subsequent military coup destabilized the situation again as Aristede was arrested and expelled from the country. This also led to massive efforts by Haitian citizens to flee the country in makeshift boats and the deaths of hundreds attempting to reach the United States.

The situation had been brought to the attention of the United Nations as early as 1991 but no action occurred until the MICIVIH was deployed in early 1993, followed by the establishment of the United Nations Mission in Haiti (UNMIH). The Haitian Government was initially hostile to both missions and failed to live up to interim agreements that would return President Aristede to power and allow Haiti to transition to a truly democratic society. In response, the UN brought additional pressure to bear in October 1993 when extensive international embargoes were placed on oil and arms imports. When it became obvious that the sanctions were having little effect, a naval blockade was imposed and, after 60 years, United States Marines prepared to return to the island of Haiti in force. This invasion was averted when the military leaders of the Haitian Government, in September 1994, agreed to step down, thus paving the way for the return of the legally-elected President Aristede to office. UNMIH assumed responsibility for the peace-keeping effort in March 1995 and supervised the general elections held later that year. With most of UNMIH's goals achieved, the mission was terminated in June 1996.

On July 1 1996, UNMIH was replaced by a smaller successor mission, the United Nations Support Mission in Haiti (UNSMIH) with virtually the same mandate but with emphasis on the training of a professional police force and providing assistance in the rebuilding of the country's infrastructure. Troops assigned to the follow-on mission will be awarded the UNMIH medal with an UNSMIH clasp.

UN troops on parade during transfer ceremony marking the transfer of command from the Multinational Force to the United Nations Mission in Haiti. UN Photo.

33. UNASOG - United Nations Aouzou Strip Observer Group

NO MEDAL ISSUED

MANDATE: The briefest mission ever established by the UN Security Council was the United Nations Aouzou Strip Observer Group (UNASOG) which was deployed for a forty (40) day period between May and June of 1994. Its principal tasks were: to verify the 4 April 1994 agreement; to verify the withdrawal of Libyan administrative and military forces from the Aouzou Strip between Chad and Libya; to monitor the removal of mines from the area; to establish safe border crossing points for persons and property; to demarcate and monitor the frontier for border incursions; to encourage the maintenance of good-neighborliness and further cooperation with the United Nations team in the field.

BACKGROUND: The landlocked country of Chad is a centuries-old former kingdom in north-central Africa which had been ruled by France since the turn of the 20th century as part of French Equatorial Africa. Since achieving its independence in 1960, Chad has been plagued with a series of uprisings that saw the country see-saw between democratic and communist governments and revise its attitudes towards Libya, her neighbor to the north, as the political atmosphere changed.

It was in this climate that Libyan troops entered the country in 1980, at the request of the Government of Chad, to quell internal unrest. After accomplishing their task, the Libyan forces left in 1981. Within a few years, French troops were called upon to oppose a Libyan-backed rebellion, withdrawing in 1984. The next shift occurred in 1990, when a Libyan-supported insurgent group, the Patriotic Salvation Movement, took control of the government. However, throughout all of the upheavals, the two nations maintained a long-standing dispute over the Aouzou Strip, a mineral-rich area that lies on the border between the two countries.

Country/Location	Chad/Libyan Border
Dates	May 1994 to June 1994
Countries Participating	(6) Bangladesh, Ghana, Honduras, Kenya, Malaysia, Nigeria
Maximum Srength	9 military observers and 6 international civilian staff (1994)
Current Strength	0
Fatalities	None
Medal Number	None
CLASP(S)	None

In 1989, at the urging of many of the concerned countries in the area, Chad and Libya finally indicated their willingness to resolve the dispute over the Aouzou Strip by peaceful means. Chad's claim to the territory was governed by a treaty concluded between the French Republic and the Kingdom of Libya in 1955. Owing to the age of the document and the fact that the present disputants were entirely new countries and not signatories to the original treaty, Libya rejected the argument. After several rounds of inconclusive talks, however, the matter was submitted in 1990 to the International Court of Justice (ICJ), the principal judicial organ of the United Nations. In the Court's ruling, not delivered until early 1994, it was decreed that the original boundaries established by the 1955 treaties were valid and binding upon the all successor nations.

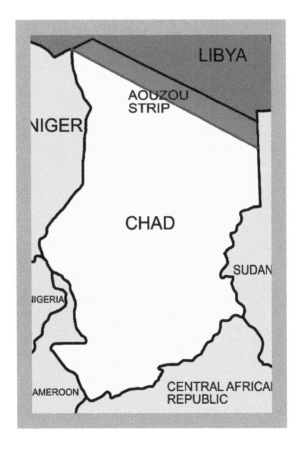

Both Governments again pledged to abide by the ICJ's decision but, to reassure all parties that its provisions were being adhered to, the United Nations established a small reconnaissance mission, followed by the UNASOG group (drawn from the nearby MINURSO operation) to verify all aspects of the agreements. The UNASOG mission accomplished all of its tasks within the prescribed 40 days and was terminated in June 1994.

34. UNMOT - United Nations Mission of Observers in Tajikistan

UNMOT The light blue edge stripes represent the United Nations and its efforts to monitor the established peace agreements and thegreen and white areas denote the flora and the snow-peaked mountains of Tajikistan.

Country/Location	Tajik-Afghan Border
Dates	December 1994 to May 2000
Countries Participating	(10) Austria, Bangladesh, Bulgaria, Denmark, Hungary, Jordan, Poland, Switzerland, Ukraine, Uruguay
Maximum Srength	84 authorized (45 military, 18 international staff, 26 local civilian staff)
Current Strength	0
Fatalities	1 (1996)
Medal Number	34
CLASP(S)	None

MANDATE: To assist the Joint Commission to monitor the implementation of the Agreement on a Temporary Cease-fire and the Cessation of Other Hostile Acts on the Tajik-Afghan border and within the country for the duration of the talks; to investigate reports of cease-fire violations, gather the facts and report them to the United Nations and to the Joint Commission; to provide its good offices as stipulated in the Agreement; to maintain close contact with the parties to the conflict, as well as close liaison with the Mission of the Conference on Security and Cooperation in Europe (CSCE) and with the collective peace-keeping forces of the Commonwealth of Independent States in Tajikistan and with the border forces; to provide support for the efforts of the Secretary-General's Special Envoy; to provide political liaison and coordination services which could facilitate expeditious humanitarian assistance by the international community.

BACKGROUND: The mountainous country of Tajikistan (spelled as Tadzhikistan in some references) is located in the southernmost portion of the former Soviet Union with the People's Republic of China to the east and Afghanistan bordering on the south. Owing to its location, at various times in its history the region found itself under the major competing influences of Western European, Asian and Islamic cultures. In this century, the Russian Revolution ultimately led to its incorporation into the Soviet Union, first as an associated province and finally as a partner state, the Tajik SSR. After the breakup of the Soviet Union in 1991, Tajikistan declared its independence and, almost immediately, was engulfed in a civil war which has resulted in thousands of deaths and nearly one million refugees and displaced persons.

The inhabitants in Tajikistan form a traditional society characterized by clan and ethnic divisions and independence gave rise to those regions and groups that had traditionally been excluded from power. The ethnic minorities, in particular the Islamic groups, began to expect a fuller participation in the affairs of the new state. As a result, in May 1992, the Tajik opposition, an informal coalition of Islamic and other minority groups, seized power thus plunging the country into civil war. The areas of the country where the clans were strongest saw little fighting but areas where the population was mixed, particularly near the Afghan border, experienced the heaviest combat. Although the insurgent groups were badly defeated and were forced across the border into neighboring Afghanistan, persistent skirmishing and raids across the border continued to destabilize the area.

After a number of attempts by other countries in the region to mediate the dispute, the United Nations sent a Special Envoy who, after a number of attempts, succeeded in getting the sides to a meeting in Teheran at which time a tentative cease-fire and provisions for monitoring and humanitarian efforts were approved. The United Nations Mission of Observers in Tajikistan (UNMOT) arose from this pact and deployed late in 1994. UN peace efforts continued until 15 May 2000 when the mandate terminated and the mission was accomplished.

UNMOT staff confer with a member of the government militia in the Garm Valley, Tajikistan UN Photo.

35. UNAVEM III - United Nations Angola Verification Mission III

UNAVEM III The light blue and white areas represent the United Nations' presence in Angola and the yellow, red and black colors are those of the Angolan flag. This is the same ribbon as the two earlier missions, UNAVEM I and UNAVEM II .

Country/Location	Angola
Dates	February 1995 to June 1997
Countries Participating	(38) Algeria, Argentina, Bangladesh, Brazil, Bulgaria, Congo, Egypt, Fiji, France, Guinea-Bissau, Hungary, India, Italy, Jordan, Kenya, Korean Republic, Malaysia, Mali, Morocco, Namibia, Netherlands, New Zealand, Nigeria, Norway, Pakistan, Poland, Portugal, Romania, Russian Federation, Senegal, Slovakia, Sweden, Tanzania, Ukraine, United Kingdom, Uruguay, Zambia, Zimbabwe
Maximum Srength	8,405 authorized (350 military observers, 7,000 troops and support personnel, 260 police observers plus provisions for 420 international civilian staff, 300 locally-recruited staff and 75 UN Volunteers)
Current Strength	0
Fatalities	33
Medal Number	35
CLASP(S)	None

MANDATE: Established to assist the Government of Angola and the União Nacional para a Independência Accordos de Paz signed on 31 May 1991, the Lusaka Protocol signed on 20 November 1994 and relevant Security Council resolutions. Among the main features of UNAVEM III's mandate were the following: to provide good offices and mediation to the Angolan parties; to monitor and verify the extension of State administration throughout the country and the process of national reconciliation; to supervise, control and verify the disengagement of forces and to monitor the cease-fire; to verify information received from the Government and UNITA regarding their forces, as well as all troop movements; to assist in the establishment of quartering areas; to verify the withdrawal, quartering and demobilization of UNITA forces; to supervise the collection and storage of UNITA armaments; to verify the movement to barracks and the completion of formation of Government forces; to verify the free circulation of persons and goods; to verify and monitor the neutrality of the Angolan National Police, the disarming of civilians, the quartering of rapid-reaction police and security arrangements for UNITA leaders; to coordinate, facilitate and support humanitarian activities directly linked to the peace process as well as participating in mine-clearance activities; to declare formally that all essential requirements for the holding of the second round of presidential elections have been fulfilled and to support, verify and monitor the electoral process.

BACKGROUND: In early 1995, a general lessening of internal tensions in the country had resulted from agreements by both parties to honor the 1991 Accordos de Paz (Peace Accords) and the 1994 Lusaka Protocol. Also at this time, the UNAVEM II mission, whose role had always been passive ("observe and report"), was approaching the expiration of its original mandate. Since massive new efforts were planned in the general areas of disarmament, personal freedoms, national security and humanitarian aid, the United Nations decided to replace the UNAVEM II mission with a newer, larger force which would be capable of assisting in those areas where the local government was incapable or unwilling to provide the necessary manpower. The third United Nations Angola Verification Mission (UNAVEM III) was instituted with an eight-fold increase in manpower, vastly widened areas of responsibilities and a series of assignments within its mandate that were in effect until June 1997.

Brazilian Troops on Parade in Angola. UN Photo.

36. UNPREDEP - United Nations Preventive Deployment Force

UNPREDEP *The ribbon has wide edges of light blue with narrow stripes of white which represent the United Nations and its basic objective of peace. The red and yellow stripes and the red center denote the UNPREDEP Command and its mission in Macedonia as well as colors of the flag and coat-of-arms of that former state (a golden lion on a field of red).*

Country/Location	Former Yugoslav Republic of Macedonia
Dates	March 1995 to 28 Feburary 1999
Countries Participating	(32) Argentina, Bangladesh, Belgium, Brazil, Canada, Czech Republic, Denmark, Egypt, Finland, France, Ghana, Indonesia, Ireland, Jordan, Kenya, Malaysia, Nepal, Netherlands, New Zealand, Nigeria, Norway, Pakistan, Poland, Portugal, Russian Federation, Senegal, Spain, Sweden, Switzerland, Ukraine, United Kingdom, United States
Maximum Srength	1,314 authorized (1,050 troops, 35 military observers and 26 civilian police plus provisions for 76 international staff and 127 locally-recruited civilian staff)
Current Strength	0
Fatalities	None (1996)
Medal Number	36
CLASP(S)	None

MANDATE: To monitor and report on any developments in the border areas with Albania and the Federal Republic of Yugoslavia (Serbia and Montenegro) which could undermine confidence and stability in the former Yugoslav Republic of Macedonia and threaten its territory. Its tasks included preventive deployment, good offices, measures to build confidence, early warning, fact-finding, monitoring and reporting, as well as selected developmental projects including appropriate directives of the Security Council. In addition, the mission was responsible for maintaining liaison with the host country's Ministry of Defence and relations with the General Staff of the Federal Republic of Yugoslavia as well as the relevant ministries of the neighboring country of Albania.

BACKGROUND: Established as a second offshoot of UNPROFOR, the initial United Nations mission in the Former Yugoslavia, the UNPREDEP operation concerned itself with the security of Macedonia, a mountainous region lying in the southeast and bordering Albania on the west and Greece on the east. Given the instability that was created by the disintegration of Yugoslavia, the troubles in Macedonia seemed to have been confined to cross-border smuggling of arms and supplies as well as incidents of violence between smugglers, illegal immigrants and border patrols.

Nonetheless, the threat of expansion of the ongoing wars in the other former Yugoslav states was sufficient justification to deploy the UNPREDEP mission. The military component of UNPREDEP consisted of two mechanized infantry battalions- a Nordic composite battalion and a United States Army task force- supported by a heavy engineering platoon from Indonesia. The presence and high visibility of these UN troops patrolling the northern and western borders of the country have had a calming and stabilizing effect throughout the region. In addition, the political staff attached to the mission were responsible for civil and humanitarian matters and maintained an active dialogue with all political and ethnic forces to promote internal peace and stability.

By comparison with the other UN missions in Former Yugoslavia, UNPREDEP achieved a reasonable level of success and is widely considered to be an instance of a successful deployment of UN peacekeeping forces in the prevention of conflict and violence against civilians. The operation was shut down on 28 February 1999, after its last extension in Resolution 1186 when China vetoed its renewal in 1999 following North Macedonia's diplomatic recognition of Taiwan.

37. UNCRO - United Nations Confidence Restoration Operation in Croatia

UNCRO *The basic color of the ribbon is light blue with a central band of red, flanked by white, representing the United Nations Protected Areas. On the left, the stripe of green represents the forests of Yugoslavia and a band of brown on the right side represents the mountains This is the same ribbon as the UNPROFOR mission.*

Country/Location	Croatia
Dates	March 1995 to January 1996
Countries Participating	(38) Argentina, Bangladesh, Belgium, Brazil, Canada, Czech Republic, Denmark, Egypt, Estonia, Finland, France, Germany, Ghana, Indonesia, Ireland, Jordan, Kenya, Lithuania, Malaysia, Nepal, Netherlands, New Zealand, Nigeria, Norway, Pakistan, Poland, Portugal, Russian Federation, Senegal, Slovakia, Spain, Sweden, Switzerland, Tunisia, Turkey, Ukraine, United Kingdom, United States
Maximum Srength	15,522 (includes 14,663 troops, 328 military observers and 531 civilian police) (1995)
Current Strength	0
Fatalities	16
Medal Number	37
CLASP(S)	None

MANDATE: To perform the functions envisaged in the cease-fire agreement of 29 March 1994; to facilitate implementation of the economic agreement of 2 December 1994; to facilitate implementation of all relevant Security Council resolutions; to assist in controlling, by monitoring and reporting, the crossing of military personnel, equipment, supplies and weapons over the international borders between Croatia and Bosnia and Herzegovina and Croatia and the Federal Republic of Yugoslavia (Serbia and Montenegro) at the border crossings; to facilitate the delivery of international humanitarian assistance to Bosnia and Herzegovina through the territory of Croatia and to monitor the demilitarization of the Prevlaka peninsula.

BACKGROUND: By late 1995, with the widening and deepening of the internal conflicts in the former Republic of Yugoslavia, the various peace-keeping tasks of the United Nations could no longer be administered under the single command of UNPROFOR. The number of separate ethnic and national interests involved virtually demanded that smaller, more manageable jurisdictions be established if a workable cease-fire and a lasting peace were to be achieved. For this reason, on 31 March 1995, the UN established the United Nations Confidence Restoration Operation (UNCRO) as one half of the replacement for the UNPROFOR mission (the other half being the UNPREDEP operation). As a result, UN troops and observers were deployed in Serb-controlled Western Slavonia, the Krajina region and Eastern Slavonia and additional observers were stationed in the Prevlaka Peninsula. It was decided that UNCRO should be an interim arrangement to create the conditions that would facilitate a negotiated settlement consistent with the territorial integrity of Croatia and guarantee the security and rights of all communities living in Croatia.

Croatia's reintegration by force of Western Slavonia and the Krijina region in mid-1995 effectively eliminated the need for

United Nations troops in those areas and they were promptly withdrawn. However, in Eastern Slavonia- the last Serb-controlled territory in Croatia- the mandate of UNCRO remained essentially unchanged. At the urging of the UN, the Government of Croatia and the Croatian Serb leadership agreed to resolve the issue of Eastern Slavonia through negotiation. The UN-sponsored talks concluded with the signing of the Basic Agreement on the Region of Eastern Slavonia, Baranja and Western Sirmium on 12 November 1995. The agreement called for the peaceful integration of the specified regions into Croatia and requested the UN to establish a transitional authority to administer the region in the interim. Once that was accomplished, UNCRO was terminated and, once again, two follow-on missions (UNTAES, pg. 71 and UNMOP, pg. 73) were established.

Canadian soldiers evacuate a casualty. UN Photo

38. UNMIBH - United Nations Mission in Bosnia and Herzegovina

UNMIBH Originally the same as the UNPROFOR ribbon (no. --), the design was recently changed. In the new ribbon, the light blue and white represent the UN's presence and the universal hope for peace, the light green represents the forests of Bosnia Herzegovina in spring and the red denotes the sunrise over the country's mountains.

Country/Location	Bosnia and Herzegovina
Dates	December 1995 to 31 December 2002
Countries Participating	(35) Argentina, Austria, Bangladesh, Bulgaria, Denmark, Egypt, Estonia, Fiji, Finland, France, Germany, Ghana, Greece, Hungary, India, Indonesia, Ireland, Jordan, Kenya, Malaysia, Nepal, Netherlands, Norway, Pakistan, Poland, Portugal, Russian Federation, Senegal, Spain, Sweden, Switzerland, Tunisia, Turkey, Ukraine, United States
Maximum Srength	3,006 authorized (1,721 police monitors, 5 military liaison officers, 380 international staff and 900 locally-recruited staff)
Current Strength	0
Fatalities	12 (2002)
Medal Number	38
CLASP(S)	None

MANDATE: The mission tasks included (a) monitoring, observing and inspecting law enforcement activities and facilities, including associated judicial organizations, structures and proceedings, (b) advising law enforcement personnel and forces, (c) training law enforcement personnel, (d) facilitating, within the mission of assistance, the parties' law enforcement activities, (e) assessing threats to public order and advising on the capabilities of law enforcement agencies to deal with such threats, (f) advising government authorities in Bosnia and Herzegovina on the organization of effective civilian law enforcement agencies and (g) assisting by accompanying the parties' law enforcement personnel as they carry out their responsibilities. In addition, the mission was to consider requests for assistance from the parties or law enforcement agencies in Bosnia and Herzegovina with priority being given to ensuring the existence of conditions for free and fair elections.

BACKGROUND: The territory known as Bosnia and Herzegovina within the former State of Yugoslavia has known its share of political unrest, ethnic hatreds and factional disturbances since it was part of the Ottoman Empire in the 17th century. Under the rule of the Ottoman Turks, most of the population converted to Islam, a factor which was to play a major role in the years to come. By the early 20th century, with Turkish rule on the decline, the region was annexed by Austria-Hungary setting off a major international crisis. The action outraged Russia, Turkey and nearby Serbia but all actions ceased when Austria's powerful

ally, Germany, threatened to invade the Balkans. The area lived up to its reputation as the "Powderkeg of Europe" in 1914 when Austrian Archduke Ferdinand, on a diplomatic fence-mending visit to Sarajevo, was assassinated by a Bosnian Serb thus precipitating World War I. The war resulted in the formation of the Kingdom of the Serbs, Croats and Slovenes and the ultimate annexation of Bosnia and Herzegovina into the loose federation.

Subsequent to World War II, the new kingdom fell under communist rule and the Federation of Yugoslavia was formed. With the collapse of communist rule in 1989-90, Bosnia and Herzegovina were engulfed in a wave of nationalism that swept Yugoslavia. After Croatia quit the federation in 1991, Bosnian Croats and Muslims called for an independent, multinational republic. Bosnian Serbs, however, refused to secede from Yugoslavia and, by 1992, Bosnia and Herzegovina were wracked by a civil war of staggering brutality in which entire populations were systematically and ruthlessly "cleansed" from areas taken over by each ethnic group. With the Dayton Accords in 1995, the responsibility for bringing peace to the region was assumed by the North Atlantic Treaty Organization and troops from its member nations, France, Great Britain and the United States. The United Nations Mission in Bosnia and Herzegovina (UNMIBH) was created as an adjunct to NATO peace-keeping efforts to coordinate civilian activities of the peace settlement and remained in place until December of 2002.

39. UNTAES - United Nations Transitional Administration for Eastern Slavonia, Baranja and Western Sirmium

UNTAES The basic color of the ribbon is light blue with a central band of red, flanked by white, representing the United Nations Peace Forces. On the left, the stripe of green represents the forests of Yugoslavia and the band of yellow on the right represents the hope for the lush cornfields which grow in peaceful times.

Country/Location	Northeast portion of Croatia (Former Yugoslavia)
Dates	January 1996 to 15 January 1998
Countries Participating	(33) Argentina, Bangladesh, Belgium, Brazil, Canada, Czech Republic, Denmark, Egypt, Fiji, Finland, France, Ghana, Indonesia, Ireland, Jordan, Kenya, Nepal, Netherlands, New Zealand, Nigeria, Norway, Pakistan, Poland, Portugal, Russian Federation, Senegal, Slovakia, Sweden, Switzerland, Tunisia, Turkey, Ukraine, United Kingdom
Maximum Srength	5,000 troops, 600 civilian police and 100 military observers plus civil affairs and administrative components.
Current Strength	0
Fatalities	2 (1996)
Medal Number	39
CLASP(S)	None

MANDATE: The UNTAES mission was established in 1996 to supervise and help in the demilitarization of the region as provided for in the Basic Agreement to be carried out by the parties within 30 days of the full deployment of UNTAES, to oversee the return of refugees and displaced persons to their homes, to establish and train a temporary police force to build professionalism among the police and confidence among all ethnic communities, to monitor the treatment of offenders and the prison system, to organize elections for all local government bodies, to maintain monitors along the international borders of the region to facilitate the free movement of persons across existing borders, to restore the normal functioning of all public services in the region without delay, to monitor the parties' commitment to respect human rights and fundamental freedoms, to cooperate with the International Tribunal for the Former Yugoslavia in its task of investigating and prosecuting war crimes and promote the realization of the commitments made in the Basic Agreement between Croatia and local Serb authorities and contribute to the overall maintenance of peace and security.

BACKGROUND: As part of the United Nations' effort to compartmentalize the terrible internal strife in the Former Yugoslavia to deal with local issues more effectively, the mission designated as UNTAES was established in early 1996 to deal with the ethnic difficulties in the provinces of Eastern Slavonia, Baranja and Western Sirmium (also known as Western Srem).

The disputes originated in 1991 when Croatia declared her independence from the Socialist Federal Republic of Yugoslavia. Serb forces immediately seized about 30 percent of Croatia's territory including the three provinces covered by this

mission. However, these regions remained in Serb hands after a major military offensive in August 1995, which saw the Croats retake most of the Serb-held territory. As a consequence, some 150,000 refugees were created in a massive change in the region's demographic composition.

After intense diplomatic negotiations arranged by the United Nations, a Basic Agreement was signed by the Presidents of Croatia and Serbia establishing the UNTAES mission and designating the area as part of Croatia as soon as the civil and military objectives of UNTAES were accomplished.   Among these are the training of the first groups of police officers, the re-opening of the Zagreb-Belgrade highway which cuts through the UNTAES mission area, the opening of the Adriatic pipeline from Croatia to the Federal Republic of Yugoslavia and the resumption of mail and telephone service between the mission area and Croatia after four years.

UNTAES got off to a good start. The United Nations Security Council Resolution 1145 in late 1997 arranged for the United Nations Police Support Group (UNPSG) to take over UNTAES' policing tasks, effectively concluding the UNTAES mission on January 15, 1998.

A support group of 180 civilian UN police officers remained to monitor the progress of the Croatian police and oversee the return of the refugees. As additional help to UNTAES mission, Organization for Security and Cooperation in Europe established OSCE Mission to Croatia whose tasks was to overlook of respect of human and minority rights, return of refugees, formation of public institutions and monitoring of work of civil police.

40. UNSMIH - United Nations Support Mission in Haiti

UNSMIH The ribbon center is designed with the half blue-half red design of the flag of the Republic of Haiti and the white and light blue edge stripes denote friendship. This is the same ribbon as the UNMIH mission but is worn with a clasp, UNSMIH.

Country/Location	Haiti
Dates	July 1996 to July 1997
Countries Participating	(4) providing military assistance: Bangladesh, Canada, Pakistan, Trinidad and Tobago; (7) providing civilian police components: Algeria, Canada, Djibouti, France, Mali, Russian Federation, Togo
Maximum Srength	1,300 military personnel, 300 civilian police plus approximately 400 local staff
Current Strength	0
Fatalities	1
Medal Number	40
CLASP(S)	UNSMIH

MANDATE: Continues the mandate of the previously-deployed UNMIH mission in the country of Haiti. With the termination of UNMIH, the follow-on effort was expected to carry out the following tasks:

- Assist the Government of Haiti in the professionalization of the police force,
- Assist the Haitian authorities in maintaining a secure and stable environment conducive to the current efforts to establish and train an effective national police force,
- Support the role of the Special Representative of the Secretary-General to coordinate United Nations activities, particularly in the areas of promoting institution-building, national reconciliation and economic rehabilitation.

BACKGROUND: In June of 1996, with the successful conclusion of national elections and the election of President Preval, the mandate of the United Nations peace-keeping effort known as UNMIH was terminated, thus bringing to a close the first phase of United Nations efforts to help the Haitian people restore democracy, stability and the rule of law in their troubled country.

Responding to a request from the new Haitian Government for additional support, the UN Secretary General proposed a new, smaller operation, the United Nations Support Mission in Haiti (UNSMIH).

The new mission's primary purpose was to help Haiti consolidate the gains already made in professionalizing the Haitian National Police (HNP) and reaffirm the desire to return the nation to a state of stability. Further efforts in this area were expected to fully establish the police force as an integral element in the consolidation of democracy and the revitalization of Haiti's justice system.

Much of the UN's effort was expected in the area of civil disobedience. Because of many years of internal neglect, the country's infrastructure, particularly roads and electrification have suffered badly. There was also the growing necessity for social services such as medical and educational facilities as well as improvements in basic living conditions. These unmet demands and heightened expectations have led to frequent demonstrations in the past and, with time, there is an increased potential for violence among the civilian population.

To guard against this possibility during the transitional rebuilding efforts, the United Nations had stepped up its efforts to train the HNP and to provide funding to renovate and revitalize the country's police stations as well as for badly-needed communications equipment. UNSMIH's mandate ran until July 1997.

UN Photo

41. UNMOP - United Nations Mission of Observers in Prevlaka

UNMOP The ribbon has medium stripes of light blue and narrower white stripes representing the United Nations and the purpose of peace. Dark blue areas represent waters surrounding the Prevlaka Peninsula and the yellow areas denote the golden sun promising a peaceful and prosperous future.

Country/Location	Prevlaka Peninsula (Croatia)
Dates	January 1996 to December 2002
Countries Participating	(27) Argentina, Bangladesh, Belgium, Brazil, Canada, Czech Republic, Denmark, Egypt, Finland, France, Ghana, Indonesia, Ireland, Jordan, Kenya, Nepal, New Zealand, Nigeria, Norway, Pakistan, Poland, Portugal, Russian Federation, Sweden, Switzerland, Ukraine, United Kingdom
Maximum Srength	28 military observers
Current Strength	0
Fatalities	None
Medal Number	41
CLASP(S)	None

MANDATE: UNMOP continued the mandate of the previously-deployed UNPROFOR mission in the strategically important Prevlaka Peninsula. It aimed to perform the functions envisaged in the cease-fire agreement of 29 March 1994; to facilitate implementation of the economic agreement of 2 December 1994; to facilitate implementation of all relevant Security Council resolutions; to assist in controlling, by monitoring and reporting, the crossing of military personnel, equipment, supplies and weapons over international borders, to facilitate the delivery of international humanitarian assistance and to monitor the demilitarization of the Prevlaka peninsula.

BACKGROUND: The United Nations Mission of Observers in Prevlaka (UNMOP) held two major distinctions in the annals of the United Nations: (1) it was the smallest observer force ever deployed for which an individual medal was authorized and (2) it was the most obscure territory to involve UN military observers (it is virtually impossible to locate on a major Atlas of the World).

The mission had its beginnings as an offshoot of the UNPROFOR operation which included many activities associated with the civil strife then occurring in Bosnia-Herzegovina, Macedonia and Croatia. In 1992, the Presidents of Croatia and the Federal Republic of Yugoslavia (Serbia and Montenegro) agreed to the formation of the UNPROFOR mission as a means to the ultimate solution to problems in territories under their control. Almost as an afterthought, the Croatia portion of UNPROFOR's operational task was extended to include monitoring of the demilitarization of the vital Prevlaka Peninsula near Dubrovnik. With the termination of UNPROFOR's activities in 1995, administrative responsibility for the Prevlaka effort passed to the short-lived UNCRO mission and, in turn, was delegated to UNMOP upon the expiration of UNCRO's mandate.

The Prevlaka operation, albeit small in scope, functioned in a positive atmosphere in stark contrast to the major trouble spots still found in the Former Yugoslavia. Some heavily-mined areas were cleared under the guidance of United Nations monitors and regular foot and vehicle patrols along the border was carried out to prevent incidents, promote confidence among the parties, reduce tensions and, of major importance, to ensure the safety of the UN military observers. In the area of actual demilitarization, Croatian military personnel were withdrawn from the area, heavy weapons removal was begun and restrictions of movement was eased on both sides of the border. Cooperation between UNMOP and the multinational implementation force (IFOR) was maintained through high level staff meetings that were held at regular intervals. After nearly five years of intense fighting, stalemate, tension and conflict, the UNMOP effort made an important contribution to the normalization and stability on the Prevlaka Peninsula. After assessing its accomplishments, the UN Security Council extended UNMOP's original three-month mandate until December 2002.

UN Photo

42. MINUGUA - United Nations Verification Mission in Guatemala

MINUGUA: The ribbon represents the colours of the Guatemala flag brought together in the center by UN blue. Qualifying time for the medal is 90 days of service in the Mission.

Country/Location	Guatemala
Dates	1997 to May, 1997
Countries Participating	Argentina, Australia, Austria, Brazil, Canada, Ecuador, Germany, Norway, Russian Federation, Singapore, Spain, Sweden, Ukraine, United States, Uruguay and Venezuela
Maximum Srength	132 military observers and 13 medical personnel
Current Strength	- 0
Fatalities	4
Medal Number	- 42
CLASP(S)	-

MANDATE: The United Nations Verification Mission in Guatemala -- the peacekeeping mission within the larger civilian and humanitarian MINUGUA mission -- was established by the Security Council in resolution 1094 (1997) on 20 January 1997 for a three-month period to verify the Agreement on the Definitive Ceasefire between the Government of Guatemala and the Unidad Revolucionaria Nacional Guatemalteca (URNG), which was signed at Oslo on 4 December 1996.

Verification functions under the Oslo Agreement included observation of a formal cessation of hostilities, the separation and concentration of the respective forces of forces, and the disarmament and demobilization of URNG combatants in assembly points specifically prepared for this purpose.

BACKGROUND: Thirty-six years of internal conflict in Guatemala came to an end on 29 December 1996 when the Government of Guatemala and the Unidad Revolucionaria Nacional Guatemalteca (URNG) signed the Agreement on a Firm and Lasting Peace. The Agreement brought into effect a number of previous agreements negotiated over a period of six years under United Nations auspices. One of those, the 1994 Comprehensive Agreement on Human Rights, was already being verified by the United Nations. At the request of the parties, and without awaiting a ceasefire and the conclusion of the negotiating process, the United Nations General Assembly), on 19 September 1994, had established the United Nations Mission for the Verification of Human Rights and of Compliance with the Commitments of the Comprehensive Agreement on Human Rights in Guatemala (MINUGUA).

The Secretary-General noted that the exemplary manner in which the Agreement on the Definitive Ceasefire had been implemented was "above all a testimony to the determination of both the Government of Guatemala and URNG to put an end to the bitter armed conflict between them". The mutual confidence gained in the joint implementation of the ceasefire was an important political capital that both parties could draw on as they faced the challenges of

reintegration and the task of implementing the other peace accords.

The Secretary-General also said that credit for the success achieved in the ceasefire process was also due to the international community which showed its own determination to put its resources and experience at the service of the demobilization of URNG combatants. He acknowledged in particular the role of the European Union, USAID, OAS and the United Nations programmes and agencies that took the lead in providing logistical and other support to the demobilization process, as well as that of the many Governments that contributed to this concerted effort.

The Secretary-General paid tribute to all the military and civilian personnel who served with distinction in the United Nations military observer group "for the successful completion of their tasks and the significant contribution they have made to the Guatemalan peace process"

Members of the Unidad Revolucionaria Nacional Guatemalteca (URNG) receiving their certificates after completing a demobilization process. UN Photo

43. MONUA Angola United Nations Observer Mission (MONUA)

MONUA   The light blue and white areas represent the United Nations' presence in Angola and the yellow, red and black colors are those of the Angolan flag. . This is the same ribbon as the original mission, UNAVEM I,II,III.

Country/Location	Angola
Dates	June 1997 to February 1999
Countries Participating	Argentina, Bangladesh, Bolivia, Brazil, Bulgaria, Congo, Egypt, France, Gambia, Ghana, Guinea Bissau, Hungary, India, Jordan, Kenya, Malaysia, Mali, Namibia, Netherlands, New Zealand, Nigeria, Norway, Pakistan, Poland, Portugal, Romania, Russian Federation, Senegal, Slovak Republic, Spain, Sweden, Tanzania, Ukraine, Uruguay, Zambia and Zimbabwe
Maximum Srength	3,026 troops and military support personnel, 253 military observers and 289 civilian police observers, supported by international and locally recruited civilian staff
Current Strength	0
Fatalities	17
Medal Number	43
CLASP(S)	None

MANDATE: MONUA was established by Security Council 30 June 1997 with an overall mandate to assist the Angolan parties in consolidating peace and national reconciliation, enhancing confidence-building and creating an environment conducive to long-term stability, democratic development and rehabilitation of the country. MONUA took over from the United Nations Verification Mission in Angola III (UNAVEM III)The Angolan Civil War raged between 1974 and 2002 and was the longest lasting conflict in Africa. Since 1988, Blue Helmets were present in Angola as observers to the conflict between the communist movement MPLA (Movimento Popular de Libertação de Angola), to which president Jose Eduardo dos Santos belongs, and the UNITA (União Nacional para a Independência Total de Angola), originally a Maoist movement.

BACKGROUND: The United Nations Observer Mission in Angola (MONUA, Mission d'Observation des Nations Unies à l'Angola) was established by United Nations Security Council Resolution 1118 of 30 June 1997. Due to the collapse of the peace process in Angola, UN Secretary General recommended to the UN Security Council that MONUA's mandate not be renewed.The mission officially terminated in on 24 February 1999, per the terms of Resolution 1213.

MONUA was the last peacekeeping mission in Angola, and was preceded by three other peacekeeping missions: UNAVEM I, II and III.

At the beginning of the mission in 1997, the UN peacekeeping force consisted of approximately 3500 soldiers, observers and police constables, coming from 17 countries. This number was reduced to 400 in 1999, when the mission ended. Seventeen Blue Helmets died in the conflict.

Since MONUA's termination, UN peacekeeping forces are no longer present in Angola.

UN member India has provided nearly 200,000 troops in support of over 40 missionsto include Angola. UN Photo

44. UNTMIH - United Nations Transition Mission in Haiti

UNTMIH The ribbon center is designed with the half blue-half red design of the flag of the Republic of Haiti and the white and light blue edge stripes denote friendship. This is the same ribbon as the UNMIH mission but is worn with a clasp, UNSMIH .

Country/Location	Haiti
Dates	August to November 1997
Countries Participating	(Argentina, Benin, Canada, France, India, Mali, Niger, Pakistan, Senegal, Togo, Tunisia, United States
Maximum Srength	250 civilian police personnel and 50 military personnel
Current Strength	0
Fatalities	None (1997)
Medal Number	44
CLASP(S)	UNSMIH

MANDATE: To assist the Government of Haiti by supporting and contributing to the professionalization of the Haitian National Police (HNP). Tasks of UNTMIH's police element included training HNP specialized units in crowd control, the rapid reaction force and Palace security, areas considered to be of distinct importance. Once reinforced, these units would considerably improve HNP's effectiveness while it pursued its own development. UNTMIH and the United Nations Development Programme continued preparation of an assistance programme to provide HNP with law enforcement expertise. Tasks of UNTMIH's military security element included ensuring, under the authority of the Force Commander, the safety and freedom of movement of United Nations personnel implementing the mandate. The Special Representative continued to coordinate the activities of the United Nations system to promote institution-building, national reconciliation and economic rehabilitation.

BACKGROUND: UNTMIH was the third in the series of United Nations peacekeeping operations in Haiti. It was established by Security Council resolution 1123 (1997) of 30 July 1997 for a single four-month period ending on 30 November 1997.

The first in the series of peacekeeping operations in Haiti was the United Nations Mission in Haiti (UNMIH), from September 1993 to June 1996. UNMIH was effectively suspended from October 1993 but was reactivated in March 1995 once a secure and stable environment had been established by the Multinational Force (September 1994--March 1995). UNMIH was succeeded in July 1996 by the United Nations Support Mission in Haiti (UNSMIH), whose mandate expired on 31 July 1997.

UNTMIH was established on the basis of a July 1997 report by the Secretary-General to the Security Council (S/1997/564). In the report, the Secretary-General stated that Haiti had taken significant strides forward. Nevertheless, the country continued to face daunting political and economic challenges. The basic consensus among Haitians for the reforms required to strengthen democratic institutions, generate economic growth and create jobs had yet to be built. Progress had also been made with regard to the establishment and training of the new police force. However, progress was slow, and the Secretary-General shared the view of Haiti's political leaders that, without steady and long-term support from the international community, the force might not be able to cope with serious incidents, risking deterioration in the security situation.

The Secretary-General shared the views expressed in November 1996 by the President of Haiti, Mr. René Préval, that a full 12 months would be necessary for the Haitian National Police (HNP) to be able to ensure a secure and stable environment without international support. Against that background, the Secretary-General recommended that the Security Council maintain United Nations support of HNP for a further period of four months, that is from July through November 1997. Were this to be agreed, the Security Council could establish a new mission to be known as the United Nations Transition Mission in Haiti (UNTMIH). The new mission would comprise both military and civilian police elements and would continue to support the Haitian authorities in the further professionalization of HNP. The Secretary-General's Special Representative would continue to coordinate activities in Haiti of the United Nations system related to institution-building, national reconciliation and economic rehabilitation.

45. MIPONUH - United Nations Civilian Police Mission in Haiti

MIPONUH The ribbon center is designed with the half blue-half red design of the flag of the Republic of Haiti and the white and light blue edge stripes denote friendship. This is the same ribbon as the UNMIH mission but is worn without a clasp.

Country/Location	Haiti
Dates	1997 to March 2000
Countries Participating	Argentina, Benin, Canada, France, India, Mali, Niger, Senegal, Togo, Tunisia, United States
Maximum Srength	300 civilian police personnel, including a special police unit, supported by a civilian establishment of some 72 international and 133 local personnel and 17 United Nations Volunteers.
Current Strength	0
Fatalities	7 police 1 other
Medal Number	45
CLASP(S)	None

MANDATE: The United Nations Civilian Police Mission in Haiti (MIPONUH) completed its mandate on 15 March 2000. Its main task was to assist the Government of Haiti in the professionalization of the Haitian National Police. MIPONUH, which succeeded the previous United Nations Missions in Haiti in December 1997, placed special emphasis on assistance at the supervisory level and on training specialized police units. Other tasks included mentoring police performance, guiding police agents in their day-to-day duties and maintaining close coordination with technical advisers to the Haitian National Police funded by the United Nations Development Programme and bilateral donors. MIPONUH's special police unit was tasked with providing assistance to MIPONUH personnel and protecting its property.

BACKGROUND: The United Nations has undertaken a number of peacekeeping missions in Haiti. The last peacekeeping mission was known as the United Nations Civilian Police Mission in Haiti (MIPONUH). Unlike the three previous missions, MIPONUH had no military component. Its mandate was to continue the work of the United Nations to support the Haitian National Police and to contribute to its professionalization.

MIPONUH was preceded by, in reverse order: the United Nations Transition Mission in Haiti (UNTMIH) (August to November 1997); the United Nations Support Mission in Haiti (UNSMIH) (July 1996 to July 1997) and the United Nations Mission in Haiti (UNMIH) (September 1993 to June 1996).

Near the end of UNTMIH's mandate, on 29 October 1997, the President of Haiti, Mr. René Préval, wrote to the Secretary-General, thanking the United Nations for its contribution to the consolidation of Haitian democracy. President Préval noted that all United Nations military forces would soon depart the country. At the same time, he said that it was important to continue working to strengthen the police force. He also expressed his confidence that Haiti would be able to continue to count on United Nations support in the new stage of its effort at national reconstruction.

MIPONUH was succeeded by the new International Civilian Support Mission in Haiti (MICAH) on 16 March 2000. The establishment of MICAH was approved by the General Assembly in resolution A/54/193 of 17 December 1999. Its mandate was to consolidate the results achieved by MIPONUH and its predecessor missions of the United Nations in Haiti as well as by the International Civilian Mission in Haiti (MICIVIH), which was a joint undertaking of the United Nations and the Organization of American States (OAS) to promote respect for human rights in Haiti. The new mission was tasked with further promoting human rights and reinforcing the institutional effectiveness of the Haitian police and the judiciary, and with coordinating and facilitating the international community's dialogue with political and social actors in Haiti.

46. UNPSG CROATIA- United Nations Police Support Group

UNPSG The ribbon : the white background represents Peace and a new beginning. In the center, a broad UN Blue band, representing the UN colors and also the Danube river which allows for the fertility of the Region. Center to left, a narrow yellow band represents the Sunflowers, so native to this land. Centered to the right a narrow dark gray band represents stone and mortar, used not only in the rebuilding of houses in this region, but in the rebuilding of the Nation.

Country/Location	Eastern Slavonia, Baranja and Western Sirmium (Danube region of Croatia)
Dates	16 January - 15 October 1998 (police monitoring handed over to OSCE on 16 October)
Countries Participating	Argentina, Austria, Denmark, Egypt, Fiji, Finland, Indonesia, Ireland, Jordan, Kenya, Lithuania, Norway, Poland, Russian Federation, Sweden, Switzerland, Ukraine, United States
Maximum Srength	114 police
Current Strength	0
Fatalities	None
Medal Number	46
CLASP(S)	None

MANDATE: Authorized by the Security Council in resolution 1145(1997) on 19 December 1997, the United Nations Police Support Group (UNPSG) took over policing tasks on 16 January 1998 from the United Nations Transitional Administration for Eastern Slavonia, Baranja and Western Sirmium UNTAES after that mission's mandate expiration. The function of the Police Support Group was to continue monitoring the performance of the Croatian police in the Danube region, particularly with respect to the return of displaced persons, for a single nine-month period beginning on 16 January 1998 and ending on 15 October 1998.

BACKGROUND: Adopting unanimously resolution on 19 December 1997, the Security Council decided to establish a support group of 180 civilian police monitors to continue monitoring the performance of the Croatian police in the Danube region, particularly with respect to the return of displaced persons, for a single nine-month period beginning on 16 January 1998. The support group was to continue that aspect of the work of the United Nations Transitional Administration for Eastern Slavonia, Baranja and Western Sirmium UNTAES.

The mandate of UNTAES expired on 15 January 1998. By that time, UNTAES had successfully accomplished its key objective under the November 1995 Basic Agreement for the region and the preceding Dayton Accords on the former Yugoslavia of peacefully reintegrating that region into Croatia within the prescribed time frame of two years. Under the Basic Agreement reached in late 1995, the Governments of Croatia and the Federal Republic of Yugoslavia, and the region's local Serb authority, had accepted a plan for the peaceful reintegration of the ethnically mixed Danube region into Croatia. The two-year transitional period ended on 15 January 1998 with the expiration of the UNTAES mandate.

The Security Council noted with concern that, despite the large presence of the Croatian police, ethnically-related incidents, evictions and housing intimidation cases had not been stopped but increased. On 26 June 1998, the Government of Croatia adopted a Programme for the Return and Accommodation of Displaced Persons, Refugees and Exiled Persons. According to the Office for Displaced Persons and Refugees, 22,501 Croatian citizens of Serb ethnicity have returned to Croatia from the Federal Republic of Yugoslavia and Bosnia and Herzegovina, and another 22,300 Croatian citizens of Serb ethnicity have returned to other parts of Croatia from the region.

The Secretary-General evaluated the overall security situation in the region as satisfactory, although a continuing and worrying trend of ethnically motivated incidents. Police performance improved notably since the beginning of the Police Support Group's mandate and the Government had taken steps to ensure that continuity. The Secretary-General stated that the conclusion of the Police Support Group's mandate marked the positive outcome of the use of civilian police personnel to ensure the consolidation of peace after the withdrawal of a much larger operation. In fulfilling its mandate, the Police Support Group helped to prevent the return of instability to the region. It proved to be a cost-effective instrument in helping to maintain conditions conducive to an orderly hand-over to OSCE pending the ultimate transfer of full responsibilities to the national Croatian authorities.

47. MINURCA United Nations Mission in the Central African Republic

MINURCA   In the center, a broad UN Blue band, representing the UN colors flanked by the colors of the Central Africa Republic Crest.

Country/Location	Central African Republic
Dates	April 1998 to February 2000
Countries Participating	Benin, Burkina Faso, Cameroon, Canada, Chad, Côte d'Ivoire, Egypt, France, Gabon, Mali, Portugal, Senegal, Togo and Tunisia
Maximum Srength	1,350 troops and military support personnel and 24 civilian police, supported by international and local civilian staff. There was also a provision for 114 international civilian staff, 111 local staff and 13 United Nations Volunteers. .
Current Strength	0
Fatalities	2 military personnel,
Medal Number	47
CLASP(S)	None

MANDATE: The United Nations Mission in the Central African Republic, more commonly known as MINURCA (which is formed from the initials of its French name Mission des Nations Unies en République Centrafricaine) was a United Nations peacekeeping force in the Central African Republic. The 1350-troop mission was established by the United Nations Security Council Resolution 1159 in March 1998. It was replaced in 2000 after the Central African Republic conducted two peaceful elections, with the entirely civilian composed UN Peace-Building Support Office in the Central African Republic (BONUCA).

BACKGROUND: Ange-Félix Patassé came to power in October 1993 following national elections; he was the first democratically elected president of the Central African Republic. He inherited a nearly bankrupt government and there was civil unrest by unpaid civil servants. Military officers were also unpaid, and some of them accused him of unequal treatment of officers from different ethnic groups. The disgruntled military officers attempted three coups in 1996. There was also widespread looting in Bangui and other provinces and the police created the Squad for the Repression of Banditry, which had the power to execute criminals the day after their apprehension.

French troops who were present in the country since its independence attempted to restore order on the President's request. In December 1996, Patassé asked the Presidents of Gabon, Burkina Faso, Chad and Mali to mediate a truce between the government and rebel forces. A peacekeeping force called Mission Interafricaine de Surveillance des Accords de Bangui (MISAB) was established to supervise the accord. The efforts were welcomed by the United Nations Security Council which authorised the presence of the force for a period of three months.

French troops temporarily supported the peacekeeping force after escalation of violence in June 1997. They however withdrew from the country in October 1997, closing their long standing military base in Bouar as well. The French troop withdrawal and their plans for stopping logistic support by April 1998 prompted the Security Council to adopt the Security Council Resolution 1159 in March 1998 which agreed to establish the United Nations Mission in the Central African Republic by 15 April 1998 to take over from MISAB

The Secretary-General stated that through their presence and active role in the Central African Republic, MINURCA, its predecessors and MISAB had provided the people and Government of the Central African Republic with much needed stability and breathing space after a period of serious upheaval. The consistent backing of the international community, as well as MINURCA's dissuasive presence and firmness in curbing threats to the country's stability, were essential for the holding of legislative and presidential elections and the launching of major political, social and economic reforms. Those positive developments took place as the wider Central African region was engulfed in violent conflict.

At the same time, the Secretary-General noted that important challenges still lay ahead for the Central African Republic. Accordingly, as the United Nations withdrew its peacekeepers from the country, the Government of the Central African Republic would need to do its utmost to build on the gains made during MINURCA's presence and continue to work resolutely towards genuine democracy and economic recovery.

48. UNOMSIL United Nations Mission in Sierra Leone

UNOMSIL The ribbon : In the center, a broad UN Blue band, flanked by stripes of light green, white and blue. The green is symbolic of the agricultural and natural resources of the country, while the white represents justice, and the blue is symbolic of Freetown's harbor.

Country/Location	Sierra Leone
Dates	JUly 1998- October 1999
Countries Participating	Bangladesh, Bolivia, Canada, China, Croatia, Egypt, Gambia, Germany, Ghana, Guinea, India, Indonesia, Jordan, Kenya, Kyrgyzstan, Malawi, Malaysia, Nepal, Nigeria, Norway, Pakistan, Russian Federation, Slovakia, Sweden, Tanzania, Ukraine, United Kingdom, Uruguay and Zambia
Maximum Srength	192 military ,192 Local staff, 24 UN Volunteers, 298 Total
Current Strength	0
Fatalities	Unknown
Medal Number	48
CLASP(S)	None

MANDATE: In February 1998, ECOMOG, responding to an attack by rebel/army junta forces, launched a military attack that led to the collapse of the junta and its expulsion from Freetown. On 10 March, President Kabbah was returned to office. The Security Council terminated the oil and arms embargo against the government and strengthened the office of the Special Envoy to include United Nations military liaison officers and security advisory personnel.

BACKGROUND: On 13 July 1998, the Security Council established the United Nations Observer Mission in Sierra Leone (UNOMSIL), with the authorized strength of 70 military observers, for an initial period of six months. The Secretary-General named Special Envoy Okelo as his Special Representative and Chief of Mission, and Brigadier-General Subhash C. Joshi (India) as Chief Military Observer. In accordance with its mandate, the mission monitored and advised efforts to disarm combatants and restructure the nation's security forces. Unarmed UNOMSIL teams, under the protection of ECOMOG, documented reports of on-going atrocities and human rights abuses committed against civilians. The Security Council was kept informed of the activities of the Mission.

Fighting continued with the rebel alliance gaining control of more than half the country. In December 1998 the alliance began an offensive to retake Freetown and in January 1999 overran most of the city. This led to the evacuation of UNOMSIL personnel to Conakry, and the subsequent downsizing of the Mission's military and civilian personnel. The Special Representative and the Chief Military Observer continued performing their duties, maintaining close contact with all parties to the conflict and monitoring the situation. Later the same month, ECOMOG troops retook the capital and again installed the civilian

government, although thousands of rebels were still reportedly hiding out in the surrounding countryside

In the aftermath of the rebel attack, Special Representative Okelo, in consultation with West African states, initiated a series of diplomatic efforts aimed at opening up dialogue with the rebels. Negotiations between the Government and the rebels began in May 1999 and on 7 July all parties to the conflict signed an agreement in Lome to end hostilies and form a government of national unity.

The Lome Peace Agreement included numerous requests for international involvement, specifically that of the United Nations, in implementing provisions contained therein, and required a substantial increase in the role of UNOMSIL.

On 20 August, the Security Council authorized the provisional expansion of UNOMSIL to up to 210 military observers along with the necessary equipment and administrative and medical support to perform the tasks of strengthening the political, civil affairs, information, human rights and child protection elements of the Mission.

On 23 September 1999, the Secretary-General recommended the Security Council authorize the deployment of the United Nations Mission in Sierra Leone (UNAMSIL), a new and significantly larger peacekeeping mission with a maximum of 6,000 military personnel, including 260 military observers, to assist in the implementation of the Lome Peace Agreement. At the same time, it decided that UNAMSIL would take over the substantive civilian and military components of UNOMSIL and that the mandate of the mission be terminated.

49 UNMIK -United Nations Interim Administration Mission in Kosovo

UNMIK *The ribbon has two outer bands of light UN blue, symbolizing the presence of the United Nations. The inner band in dark blue symbolizes the International Security presence and the cooperation and support received from it. The two bands in white symbolize the overall objective to promote peace for all the people in Kosovo.*

Country/Location	Kosovo
Dates	10 June 1999 to present
Countries Participating	Czech Republic, Ukraine, Moldova, Republic of, Rumania, Turkey, Germany, Hungary, Russian Federation, Australia
Maximum Srength	4,756 total
Current Strength	356
Fatalities	56
Medal Number	49
CLASP(S)	None

MANDATE: The United Nations Interim Administration Mission in Kosovo (UNMIK) is a mandated mission of the United Nations in Kosovo. Originally, the Security Council, by its resolution 1244 of 10 June 1999, authorized the Secretary-General to establish an international civil presence in Kosovo – the United Nations Interim Administration Mission in Kosovo (UNMIK) – in order to provide an interim administration for Kosovo under which the people of Kosovo could enjoy substantial autonomy. Its task was unprecedented in complexity and scope; the Council vested UNMIK with authority over the territory and people of Kosovo, including all legislative and executive powers and administration of the judiciary.

BACKGROUND: Subsequently, following the declaration of independence by the Kosovo authorities and the entry into force of a new constitution on 15 June 2008, the tasks of the Mission have significantly been modified to focus primarily on the promotion of security, stability and respect for human rights in Kosovo.UNMIK, a civilian mission, was in charge of the provisional administration of Kosovo with a mandate to "ensure conditions for a peaceful and normal life for all [its] inhabitants". Opinions vary, however, about how successful it was in achieving these goals.

Almost 20 years after the mission was deployed and a decade after it handed over most of its functions following Kosovo's declaration of independence and the deployment of the EU's rule-of-law mission EULEX, UNMIK's day-to-day responsibilities are now relatively minor.

Blerim Reka, a professor of international law, argued that UNMIK's mission was complete the day Kosovo declared independence on February 17, 2008, but a lack of unanimity among Security Council members meant it remained on the ground, despite its lack of powers.

"Paradoxically, the UN keeps in force a resolution which still artificially recognises the 'sovereignty' of Serbia over Kosovo, while another UN body, the International Court of Justice, has contested this resolution with its opinion from 2010,"

The International Court of Justice's advisory opinion, issued in 2010, said that Kosovo's declaration of independence did not violate Resolution 1244 because the Security Council edict did not specify Kosovo's final status.

Plans for UNMIK to hand authority over to the EULEX mission after Kosovo's constitution was approved faltered as a result of Russian opposition to Kosovo's unilateral declaration of independence. The UN Secretary-General reconfigured the mission for a temporary period. The UN will give way to the EU mission in Albanian areas, but retain control over police in Serb-inhabited areas and set up local and district courts serving minority Serbs. The move is in response to opposition to the EU presence in North Kosovo and other Serb-dominated areas. In December 2008, the European Union Rule of Law Mission in Kosovo (EULEX) assumed most of UNMIK's roles,assisting and supporting the Kosovo authorities in the rule of law area, specifically in the police, judiciary and customs areas. As of March 2011, UNMIK's work includes the overseeing the liquidation and privatization of failed businesses.

50. UNAMET United Nations Mission in East Timor

UNAMET The ribbon has two outer bands of UN blue, representing the UN presence in East Timor. There are two thin bars - a crimson bar and the bar closest to the center being sunrise yellow. These colors represent the brilliant and spectacular sunrises and sunsets experienced in East Timor. The center of the ribbon is a band of white, traditionally the color of peace and hope.

Country/Location	East Timor within the Republic of Indonesia
Dates	June - October 1999
Countries Participating	Contributions from Australia, Austria, Bangladesh, Brazil, Denmark, Ireland, Malaysia, New Zealand, Portugal, Russian Federation, Thailand, United Kingdom, Uruguay, United States
Maximum Srength	60 total uniformed personnel, 57 police,3 military liaison officers, 302 international civilian staff, 827 local civilian personnel, 124 UN Volunteers
Current Strength	0
Fatalities	None
Medal Number	50
CLASP(S)	None

MANDATE: The United Nations Mission in East Timor (UNAMET) (June - October 1999) was mandated to organize and conduct a popular consultation to ascertain whether the East Timorese people accepted a special autonomy within Indonesia or rejected the proposed special autonomy, leading to East Timor's separation from Indonesia. UNAMET was a political mission

BACKGROUND: To organise and conduct a popular consultation on the basis of a direct, secret and universal ballot, to ascertain whether the East Timorese people accept the proposed constitutional framework providing for a special autonomy for East Timor within the unitary Republic of Indonesia or reject the proposed special autonomy for East Timor, leading to East Timor's separation from Indonesia.

in 1974, Portugal sought to establish a provisional government and a popular assembly that would determine the status of East Timor. Civil war broke out between those who favoured independence and those who advocated integration with Indonesia. Unable to control the situation, Portugal withdrew. Indonesia intervened militarily and integrated East Timor as its 27th province in 1976. The United Nations never recognized this integration, and both the Security Council and the General Assembly called for Indonesia's withdrawal.

Beginning in 1982, at the request of the General Assembly, successive Secretaries-General held regular talks with Indonesia and Portugal aimed at resolving the status of the territory. In June 1998, Indonesia proposed a limited autonomy for East Timor within Indonesia. In light of this proposal, the talks made rapid progress and resulted in a set of agreements between Indonesia and Portugal, signed in New York on 5 May 1999. The two Governments entrusted the Secretary-General with organizing and conducting a "popular consultation" in order to ascertain whether the East Timorese people accepted or rejected a special autonomy for East Timor within the unitary Republic of Indonesia.

On 30 August 1999, some 98 per cent of registered East Timorese voters went to the polls deciding by a margin of 21.5 per cent to 78.5 per cent to reject the proposed autonomy and begin a process of transition towards independence.

Following the announcement of the result, pro-integration militias, at times with the support of elements of the Indonesian security forces, launched a campaign of violence, looting and arson throughout the entire territory. The Secretary-General and the Security Council undertook strenuous diplomatic efforts to halt the violence, pressing Indonesia to meet its responsibility to maintain security and order in the territory. On 12 September 1999, the Government of Indonesia agreed to accept the offer of assistance from the international community. On 25 October, the United Nations Security Council, by resolution 1272 (1999), established the United Nations Transitional Administration in East Timor (UNTAET) as an integrated, multidimensional peacekeeping operation fully responsible for the administration of East Timor during its transition to independence. The Security Council then authorized (S/RES/1264) the multinational force (INTERFET) under a unified command structure headed by a Member State (Australia) to restore peace and security in East Timor, to protect and support UNAMET in carrying out its tasks and, within force capabilities, to facilitate humanitarian assistance operations.

51. UNAMSIL - The United Nations Observer Mission in Sierra Leone

UNAMSIL The ribbon has in the center, a broad UN Blue band, flanked by stripes of light green, white and blue. The green is symbolic of the agricultural and natural resources of the country, while the white represents justice, and the blue is symbolic of Freetown's harbor.

Country/Location	Sierra Leone
Dates	1998 to 2005
Countries Participating	Bangladesh, Bolivia, Canada, China, Croatia, Egypt, Gambia, Germany, Ghana, Guinea, India, Indonesia, Jordan, Kenya, Kyrgyzstan, Malawi, Malaysia, Nepal, Nigeria, Norway, Pakistan, Russian Federation, Slovakia, Sweden, Tanzania, Ukraine, United Kingdom, Uruguay and Zambia
Maximum Srength	Military 17,500 and 170 police
Current Strength	0
Fatalities	192
Medal Number	51
CLASP(S)	None

MANDATE: The United Nations Observer Mission in Sierra Leone (UNOMSIL) was a United Nations peacekeeping operation in Sierra Leone from 1998 to 1999 with the mission to monitor the military and security situation in Sierra Leone. The mission was terminated in October 1999, when the Security Council authorized deployment of a new, and significantly larger peacekeeping operation, the Nations Mission in Sierra Leone (UNAMSIL).

BACKGROUND: On June 1998, the Security Council established the United Nations Observer Mission in Sierra Leone (UNOMSIL) for an initial period of six months. The mission monitored and advised efforts to disarm combatants and restructure the nation's security forces. Unarmed UNOMSIL teams, under the protection of ECOMOG, documented reports of on-going atrocities and human rights abuses committed against civilians.

Fighting continued with the rebel alliance gaining control of more than half the country. In December 1998 the alliance began an offensive to retake Freetown and in January overran most of the city. All UNOMSIL personnel were evacuated.

In the aftermath of the rebel attack, a series of diplomatic efforts aimed at opening up dialogue with the rebels. Negotiations led to all parties signing an agreement in Lome to end hostilities and form a government of national unity. The parties to the conflict also requested an expanded role for UNOMSILand in Oct. 1999, the Security Council authorized the establishment of UNAMSIL, a new and much larger mission with a maximum of 6,000 military personnel to assist the Government and the parties in carrying out provisions of the Lome peace agreement. At the same time, the Council decided to terminate UNOMSIL.

On 7 February 2000, the Security Council, by its resolution 1289, decided to revise the mandate of UNAMSIL to include a number of additional tasks and expand the military component to a maximum of 11,100 military personnel. In 2000 the Security Council increased the authorized strength of UNAMSIL, to 13,000 military personnel and on 30 March 2001, a further increase was authorized to 17,500 military personnel.

UNAMSIL may serve as a model for successful peacekeeping, as well as a prototype for the UN's new emphasis on peacebuilding. Over the course of its mandate, the Mission disarmed tens of thousands of ex-fighters, assisted in holding national elections, helped to rebuild the country's police force, and contributed towards rehabilitating the infrastructure and bringing government services to local communities. The United Nations also helped the Government stop illicit trading in diamonds and regulate the industry. During the war, rebels had used money from "blood" or "conflict" diamonds to buy weapons which had fueled the conflict.

UNAMSIL was not always foreseen to succeed: at one point, in May 2000, the mission nearly collapsed when the rebel Revolutionary United Front (RUF) kidnapped hundreds of peacekeepers and renounced the ceasefire in a move that endangered the credibility of UN peacekeeping. Outraged by the chaos that followed, the international community put pressure on the rebels to obey the ceasefire and slapped sanctions against RUF sponsors. Subsequently, UNAMSIL launched new mediation efforts and brought the two adversaries back to the negotiation table. It brought in more troops to monitor the cease fire and began disarming fighters from both sides. By early 2002, UNAMSIL had disarmed and demobilized more than 75,000 ex-fighters, including child soldiers. The Government declared the war officially ended. With the political situation stable, the Mission helped organize Sierra Leone 's first ever free and fair presidential and parliamentary elections by providing logistics and public information support. Two years later, the mission gave similar support for the local government elections.

52. UNTATE - United Nations Mission in East Timor

UNTATE: The ribbon has two outer bands of UN blue, representing the UN presence in East Timor. There are two thin bars - a crimson bar and the bar closest to the center being sunrise yellow. These colors represent the brilliant and spectacular sunrises and sunsets experienced in East Timor. The center of the ribbon is a band of white, traditionally the color of peace and hope.

Country/Location	Timor (New Guinea)
Dates	October, 1999 to May, 2002
Countries Participating	Australia, Bangladesh, Bolivia, Brazil, Chile, Denmark, Egypt, Fiji, Ireland, Japan, Jordan, Kenya, Malaysia, Nepal, New Zealand, Norway, Pakistan, Philippines, Portugal, Republic of Korea, Russian Federation, Singapore, Slovakia, Sweden, Thailand, Turkey, United Kingdom, United States, Uruguay. Civilian Police Personnel: Argentina, Australia, Austria, Bangladesh, Benin, Bosnia & Herzegovina, Brazil, Canada, China, Egypt, Gambia, Ghana, Jordan, Kenya, Malaysia, Mozambique, Namibia, Nepal, Niger, Nigeria, Norway, Pakistan, Philippines, Portugal, Russian Federation, Samoa, Senegal, Singapore, Slovenia, Spain, Sri Lanka, Sweden, Thailand, Turkey, Ukraine, United Kingdom, United States, Vanuatu, Zimbabwe
Maximum Srength	6,281 troops, 1,288 police and 118 military observers
Current Strength	0
Fatalities	26
Medal Number	52
CLASP(S)	None

MANDATE: The United Nations Transitional Administration in East Timor (UNTAET) provided an interim civil administration and a peacekeeping mission in the territory of East Timor, from its establishment on 25 October 1999, until its independence on 20 May 2002.

BACKGROUND: The United Nations Transitional Administration in East Timor (UNTAET) provided an interim civil administration and a peacekeeping mission in the territory of East Timor, from its establishment on 25 October 1999, until its independence on 20 May 2002, following the outcome of the East Timor Special Autonomy Referendum. Security Council Resolution 1272 established the transitional administration in 1999, and its responsibilities included providing a peacekeeping force to maintain security and order; facilitating and co-ordinating relief assistance to the East Timorese; facilitating emergency rehabilitation of physical infrastructure; administering East Timor and creating structures for sustainable governance and the rule of law; and assisting in the drafting of a new constitution and conducting elections.

UNTAET was established on 25 October 1999, and was abolished on 20 May 2002, with most functions passed to the East Timor government. After the elections for independence, pro-integration militias, at times with the support of elements of the Indonesian security forces, launched a campaign of violence, looting and arson throughout the entire territory. Many East Timorese were killed and as many as 500,000 were displaced from their homes, about half leaving the territory, in some cases by force. The Security Council then authorized the multinational force (INTERFET) under a unified command structure headed by a Member State (Australia) to restore peace and security in East Timor, to protect and support UNAMET in carrying out its tasks and, within force capabilities, to facilitate humanitarian assistance operations. Relief workers and supplies were deployed incrementally as the security situation improved. At the same time, increasing attention was paid to the voluntary repatriation of some 250,000 East Timorese from West Timor and other areas in Indonesia and the region.

Following the outbreak of violence, the Indonesian Armed Forces and police began a drawdown, eventually leaving the territory completely. Indonesian administrative officials also left. UNAMET re-established its headquarters in Dili and immediately began to restore the mission's logistical capacity and redeploy UNAMET personnel.

Meanwhile, during the first six months of 2000, more than 167,000 refugees returned from Indonesia, primarily from West Timor, with an estimated 85,000 to 120,000 remaining in camps in West Timor. The United Nations Security Council called on Indonesia to take immediate steps, in fulfillment of its responsibilities, to disarm and disband militia immediately, restore law and order in the affected areas in West Timor, ensure safety and security in the refugee camps , and prevent cross-border incursions into East Timor.

On 30 August 2001, two years after the Popular Consultation, more than 91 per cent of East Timor's eligible voters elected an 88-member Constituent Assembly tasked with writing and adopting a new Constitution and establishing the framework for future elections and a transition to full independence. The military and police forces were transferred to the newly created United Nations Mission of Support to East Timor (UNMISET).

53. MONUC - United Nations Organization Mission in the Democratic Republic of the Congo

MONUC: The ribbon has two outer bands of UN blue, representing the UN presence in the Democratic Republic of Congo (DRC). Inside the two bands, there are two equal bars in yellow that represent the dawn of peace and prosperity. The dark blue in the middle of the yellow represents the Conge river.

Country/Location	Congo
Dates	November 1999 to June, 2010
Countries Participating	Algeria, Argentina, Bangladesh, Belgium, Benin, Bolivia, Bosnia and Herzegovina, Burkina Faso, Cameroon, Canada, Central African Republic, Chad, Chile, China, Cote d'Ivoire, Czech Republic, Denmark, Egypt, El Salvador, France, Ghana, Guatemala, Guinea, India, Indonesia, Ireland, Italy, Jordan, Kenya, Libya, Madagascar, Malawi, Malaysia, Mali, Mongolia, Morocco, Mozambique, Nepal, Netherlands, Niger, Nigeria, Norway, Pakistan, Paraguay, Peru, Portugal, Romania, Russia/ Russian Federation, Senegal, Serbia, Serbia and Montenegro, South Africa, Spain, Sri Lanka, Sweden, Switzerland, Tanzania, Togo, Tunisia, Turkey, Ukraine, United Kingdom, United States of America, Uruguay, Vanuatu, Yemen and Zambia. Police personnel: Argentina, Benin, Burkina Faso, Bangladesh, Cameroon, Canada, Central African Republic, Chad, Egypt, France, Guinea, India, Italy, Ivory Coast, Jordan, Madagascar, Mali, Morocco, Nepal, Niger, Nigeria, Pakistan, Romania, Russian Federation, Senegal, Spain, Sweden, Switzerland, Togo, Turkey, Ukraine, Uruguay, Vanuatu and Yemen.
Maximum Srength	18,653 troops , 704 military observers 1,229 police
Current Strength	0
Fatalities	161
Medal Number	53
CLASP(S)	None

MANDATE: MONUC had an authorized strength of up to 5,537 military personnel, including up to 500 observers, or more, provided that the Secretary General determined that there was a need and that it could be accommodated within the overall force size and structure, and appropriate civilian support staff in the areas, inter alia, of human rights, humanitarian affairs, public information, child protection, political affairs, medical and administrative support. MONUC, in cooperation with the Joint Military Commission (JMC), had the following mandate: Protection of civilians, humanitarian personnel and United Nations personnel and facilities.

Disarmament, demobilization, monitoring of resources of foreign and Congolese armed groups.

Training and mentoring of FARDC Forces armées de la république démocratique du Congo [FARDC] in support for security sector reform

Territorial security of the Democratic Republic of the Congo.

Transition of the Mission

BACKGROUND: Extending the mandate of MONUC for the last time until 30 June 2010, the Security Council, by its resolution 1925 of 28 May 2010 decided that from 1 July it would bear the

title "United Nations Organization Stabilization Mission in the Democratic Republic of the Congo (MONUSCO)", in view of the new phase reached in the country.

Following the 1994 genocide in Rwanda and the establishment of a new government there, some 1.2 million Rwandese Hutus — including elements who had taken part in the genocide — fled to the neighbouring Kivu regions of eastern DRC, formerly Zaïre, an area inhabited by ethnic Tutsis and others. A rebellion began there in 1996, pitting the forces led by Laurent Désiré Kabila against the army of President Mobutu Sese Seko. Kabila's forces, aided by Rwanda and Uganda, took the capital city of Kinshasa in 1997 and renamed the country the Democratic Republic of the Congo (DRC).

In 1998, a rebellion against the Kabila government started in the Kivu regions. Within weeks, the rebels had seized large areas of the country. Angola, Chad, Namibia and Zimbabwe promised President Kabila military support, but the rebels maintained their grip on the eastern regions. Rwanda and Uganda supported the rebel movement, the Congolese Rally for Democracy (RCD). The Security Council called for a ceasefire and the withdrawal of foreign forces, and urged states not to interfere in the country's internal affairs.

The signing of the Lusaka Ceasefire Agreement in July 1999 between the Democratic Republic of the Congo (DRC) (cont.)

A MONUSCO APC is greeted by FARDC soldiers on their way back from the front line in the Beni region of the DRC where the UN is backing Forces armées de la république démocratique du Congo [FARDC] in an operation against Allied Decocratic Forces (ADF) militia. UN Photo

and five regional States (Angola, Namibia, Rwanda, Uganda and Zimbabwe) in July 1999 led the Security Council to establish the United Nations Organization Mission in the Democratic Republic of the Congo (MONUC). The UN resolution 1279 of 30 November 1999, initially planned for the observation of the ceasefire and disengagement of forces while maintaining liaison with all parties to the Ceasefire Agreement. Later in a series of resolutions, the Council expanded the mandate of MONUC to the supervision of the implementation of the Ceasefire Agreement and assigned multiple additional tasks.

The country's first free and fair elections in 46 years were held on 30 July 2006, with voters electing a 500-seat National Assembly. Following a run-off election for the presidency on 29 October, and resolution of a subsequent legal challenge, President Joseph Kabila (son of late Laurent Désiré Kabila assassinated in 2001) was declared the winner. The entire electoral process represented one of the most complex votes the United Nations had ever helped organize.

Following the elections, MONUC remained on the ground and continued to implement multiple political, military, rule of law and capacity-building tasks as mandated by the Security Council resolutions, including trying to resolve ongoing conflicts in a number of the DRC provinces.

On 1 July 2010, the Security Council renamed MONUC the United Nations Organization Stabilization Mission in the Democratic Republic of the Congo (MONUSCO) to reflect the new phase reached in the country.

The new mission had been authorized to use all necessary means to carry out its mandate relating, among other things, to the protection of civilians, humanitarian personnel and human rights defenders under imminent threat of physical violence and to support the Government of the DRC in its stabilization and peace consolidation efforts.

The Council decided that MONUSCO would comprise, in addition to the appropriate civilian, judiciary and correction components, a maximum of 19,815 military personnel, 760 military observers, 391 police personnel and 1,050 members of formed police units. Future reconfigurations of MONUSCO would be determined as the situation evolved on the ground, including: the completion of ongoing military operations in North and South Kivu as well as the Orientale provinces; improved government capacity to protect the population effectively; and the consolidation of state authority throughout the territory.

Soldiers from Napal provide medical aid. UN Photo

54. MICAH - International Civilian Support Mission in Haiti

MICAH: The ribbon center is designed with the half blue-half red design of the flag of the Republic of Haiti and the white and light blue edge stripes denote friendship. This is the same ribbon as the UNMIH mission (page 64) but is worn with out a clasp.

Country/Location	Haiti
Dates	The initial mandate of MICAH would start at the closing of the MIPONUH mandate and continue until 6 February 2001
Countries Participating	International staff
Maximum Srength	38 posts for internationally recruited staff (34 Professional, 2 Field Service and 2 General Service posts), 45 Local level posts and 6 United Nations Volunteers.
Current Strength	0
Fatalities	None
Medal Number	54
CLASP(S)	None

MANDATE: The International Civilian Support Mission in Haiti (MICAH) was a peacebuilding mission created by a consensus vote of the General Assembly in resolution A/54/193 of 17 December 1999. MICAH was known in French as Mission Civile Internationale d'Appui en Haiti. It was supported by the United Nations Secretary-General's Group of Friends of Haiti.

BACKGROUND: Launched on 16 March 2000, MICAH was mandated to consolidate the results achieved by MIPONUH and its predecessor missions. It was tasked with further promoting human rights and reinforcing the institutional effectiveness of the Haitian police and the judiciary, and with coordinating and facilitating the international community's dialogue with political and social actors in Haiti. MICAH formulated three pillars to carry out its mandate: the Justice Pillar, the Police Pillar, and the Human Rights Pillar.

MICAH's mandate expired on 6 February 2001.

According to the statement of the Secretary-General the new mission would be a special political mission, with a substantial technical cooperation element attached and having no peacekeeping elements The proposed staffing of MICAH would be supplemented by international and local experts for its technical assistance component in order to provide advisory services and training and to assist in capacity- building in the areas of justice, police and human rights.

Alfredo Lopes Cabral of Guinea-Bissau served as Representative of the Secretary-General (RSG) for the duration of the mission.
UN Photo

55. UNMEE - United Nations Mission in Ethiopia and Eritrea

UNMEE: The ribbon has two outer bands of UN blue, symbolizing the presence of the United Nations. The inner band in green symbolizes hope and fertility of the land. The two bands in tan symbolize religious freedom and the ruggedness of the country.

Country/Location	Asmara, Eritrea and Addis Ababa, Ethiopia
Dates	1 July 2000 to 31 July 2008
Countries Participating	Algeria, Australia, Austria, Bangladesh, Benin, Bolivia, Bosnia and Herzegovina, Brazil, Bulgaria, Canada, China, Croatia, Czech Republic, Denmark, Finland, France, Gambia, Germany, Ghana, Greece, Guatemala, India, Iran, Ireland, Italy, Jordan, Kenya, Kyrgyzstan, Malaysia, Mongolia, Namibia, Nepal, Netherlands, Nigeria, Norway, Pakistan, Paraguay, Peru, Poland, Romania, Russian Federation, Singapore, Slovakia, South Africa, Spain, Sri Lanka, Sweden, Switzerland, Tanzania, Tunisia, Ukraine, United Kingdom, United States, Uruguay and Zambia.
Maximum Srength	4,154 total uniformed personnel including 3,940 troops and 214 police supported by 229 international civilian personnel and 244 local civilian staff
Current Strength	0
Fatalities	13 military personnel, 3 international civilian personnel, 4 local civilian personnel
Medal Number	55
CLASP(S)	None

MANDATE: The United Nations Mission in Ethiopia and Eritrea (UNMEE) was established by the United Nations Security Council in July 2000 to monitor a ceasefire in the border war that began in 1998 between Ethiopia and Eritrea. The first military troops were a Netherlands and Canadian battalion 'NECBAT' who arrived and established bases in the region in December 2000.

BACKGROUND: The mission was put in place in order to formally demarcate the border between the two countries. The border followed the route as declared by an international commission in The Hague but Ethiopia refused to accept the ruling, despite originally agreeing to binding arbitration.

The mission maintained headquarters in Asmara (Eritrea), and Addis Ababa (Ethiopia), and consisted of 1,676 military personnel, amid high tensions between the two countries. About 1,500 of these peacekeepers were from the Indian Army. In addition, there were about 147 international civilians, 202 local civilians and 67 UN Volunteers. Their area of responsibility was a buffer zone 25 kilometers (15 miles) wide on the Eritrean side of the Ethiopian-Eritrean border. There were twenty fatalities recorded: 13 military personnel, 3 international civilian personnel and 4 local civilian personnel. The approved budget for the mission between 1 July 2007 and 30 June 2008 was $118.99 million.

The border between Ethiopia and Eritrea remained closed and thousands of people lived in refugee camps while perhaps a million people remain displaced. In October 2005, the Eritrean government restricted UNMEE helicopter flights along the border and demanded the reduction of the UNMEE force by 300 staffers. Eritrea also restricted movement of ground patrols inside the buffer zone. United Nations Security Council Resolution 1640 in November 2005 threatened sanctions on both parties if there was no resolution.

In September 2007 the United Nations special envoy to the Horn of Africa warned that war could resume between Ethiopia and Eritrea over their border conflict. In November, Eritrea accepted the border line demarcated by the international boundary commission, but was rejected by Ethiopia. In January 2008 the UN extended the mandate of peacekeepers on Ethiopia-Eritrea border for six months, and UN Security Council demanded Eritrea lift fuel restrictions imposed on UN peacekeepers at the Eritrea-Ethiopia border area. Eritrea declined, saying troops must leave border, and in February the UN began pulling out the 1,700-strong peacekeeper force due to lack of fuel supplies following Eritrean government restrictions. In April, UN Secretary-General Ban Ki Moon warned of the likelihood of new war between Ethiopia and Eritrea if peacekeeping mission was withdrawn completely, and outlined options for the future of the UN mission in the two countries. In May, Eritrea called on UN to terminate the peacekeeping mission.

The mission was effectively ended 31 July 2008 by a UNSC resolution adopted on 30 July 2008. Peacekeepers had been driven from the border zone by Eritrea by February 2008, and Ethiopia had refused to accept a binding International Court of Justice ruling on the border issue. There are fears that this may set a precedent to show that a country can force out UN peacekeepers. Finally there was a Eritrea–Ethiopia summit on 9 July 2018, where an agreement was signed which demarcated the border and agreed a resumption of diplomatic relations.

56. UNMISET - The United Nations Mission of Support in East Timor

UNMISET: The ribbon has two outer bands of UN blue, representing the UN presence in East Timor. Inside these two bands, there are two equal bars: the first bar is crimson and the bar closest to the center is sunrise yellow. These colors stripes represent the brilliant and spectacular sunrises and sunsets experienced in East Timor. The center of the ribbon is a band of white, traditionally the colour of peace and hope.

Country/Location	Timor (New Guinea)
Dates	20 May 2002 to 20 May 2005
Countries Participating	Argentina, Australia, Austria, Bangladesh, Benin, Bolivia, Bosnia and Herzegovina, Brazil, Bulgaria, Canada, Chile, China, Croatia, Denmark, Egypt, Fiji, Gambia, Ghana, Ireland, Japan, Jordan, Kenya, Malaysia, Mozambique, Namibia, Nepal, New Zealand, Niger, Nigeria, Norway, Pakistan, Peru, Philippines, Portugal, Republic of Korea, Russian Federation, Samoa, Senegal, Serbia and Montenegro, Singapore, Slovakia, Slovenia, Spain, Sri Lanka, Sweden, Thailand, Turkey, Ukraine, United Kingdom, United States of America, Uruguay, Vanuatu, Zambia and Zimbabwe
Maximum Srength	4,776; UN police: 771; international civilian: 465; local civilian: 856
Current Strength	0
Fatalities	2 military observers, 2 international staff,4 local civilian staff , 2 other.
Medal Number	56
CLASP(S)	None

MANDATE: The United Nations Mission of Support in East Timor (UNMISET) was established by Security Council resolution 1410 (2002) of 17 May for an initial period of 12 months, starting on 20 May 2002, with the following mandate:

To provide assistance to core administrative structures critical to the viability and political stability of East Timor;

To provide interim law enforcement and public security and to assist in the development of a new law enforcement agency in East Timor, the East Timor Police Service (ETPS). Newly independent East Timor swore in its first government and held an inaugural session of Parliament on the morning of 20 May just hours after more than 120,000 people celebrated the birth of the nation at a massive ceremony on the outskirts of Dili. The government, composed primarily of the same cabinet members that comprised the pre-independence Council of Ministers, was officially inaugurated by President Xanana Gusmão. The ceremony was attended by some 300 dignitaries including United Nations Secretary-General Kofi Annan, who handed over authority from the United Nations to the Speaker of East Timor's National Parliament. East Timor's Parliament then held its first session at which President Gusmão presented Secretary-General Annan with a request from East Timor to join the United Nations.

BACKGROUND: UNMISET and Post-independence Period UN involvement in Timor-Leste continued after its independence in May 2002 to ensure the security and stability of the nascent State. A new mission, known as the United Nations Mission of Support in East Timor (UNMISET), was set up by resolution 1410 (2002) unanimously adopted by the Security Council on 17 May 2002.

The Council decided that the Mission, to be headed by a Special Representative of the Secretary-General, would initially comprise 1,250 civilian police and an initial military troop strength of 5,000, including 120 military observers. The civilian component would include focal points for gender and HIV/AIDS, a Civilian Support Group of up to 100 personnel filling core functions, a Serious Crimes Unit and a Human Rights Unit.

The Council decided that downsizing of UNMISET should proceed as quickly as possible, and that the Mission would, over a period of two years, fully devolve all operational responsibilities to the East Timorese authorities.

Over the course of next two years, UNMISET gradually handed over its executive authority for external and internal security to the Government of Timor-Leste. In the consolidation phase of UNMISET's mandate, which lasted nine months, the mission focused on supporting the Government in building institutional capacity and ensuring the smooth transition from peacekeeping.

The mandate of UNMISET was completed in May 2005 and a successor UN political mission—the United Nations Office in Timor-Leste (UNOTIL)—was established on 20 May 2005. However, a series of events culminating in a political, humanitarian and security crisis of major dimensions led the Council to prolong UNOTIL's mandate and ultimately in August 2006 to establish a new mission—the United Nations Integrated Mission in Timor-Leste (UNMIT)to contribute to the maintenance of the external and internal security of East Timor .

57. UNMIL - United Nations Mission in Liberia

UNMIL: The ribbon has a outside stripes of United Nations blue flanked by white stripes on either side representing peace. The red stripe represents the sacrifice of human blood in the terrible carnage. In the center there is a stripe of deep blue representing the Atlantic Ocean. The red stripe represents the sacrifice of human blood in the terrible carnage. The colors also represent the Flag of Liberia which bears a close resemblance to the flag of the United States and has similar red and white stripes, as well as a blue square with a white star in the canton.

Country/Location	Liberia
Dates	September 2003 - 30 March 2018
Countries Participating	43 troop-contributing countries including Military personnel: Bangladesh, Benin, Bolivia, Brazil, Bulgaria, China, Croatia, Denmark, Ecuador, Egypt, Ethiopia, Finland, France, Gambia, Ghana, Indonesia, Jordan, Kyrgyzstan, Malaysia, Mali, Moldova, Namibia, Nepal, Niger, Nigeria, Pakistan, Poland, Republic of Korea, Romania, Russian Federation, Serbia, Togo, Ukraine, United States, Yemen, Germany , Myanmar, Zambia and Zimbabwe.
	Police personnel: Argentina, Bangladesh, Bosnia and Herzegovina, China, Egypt, El Salvador, Fiji, Gambia, Germany, Ghana, India, Jordan, Korea, Kenya, Kyrgyzstan, Lithuania, Namibia, Nepal, Nigeria, Norway, Poland, Romania, Russian Federation, Rwanda, Serbia, Sri Lanka, Sweden, Switzerland, Thailand, Turkey, Uganda, Ukraine, Uruguay, UK, United States, Yemen, Zambia and Zimbabwe.
Maximum Srength	15,000 United Nations military personnel, including up to 250 military observers and 160 staff officers, and up to 1,115 UN police officers
Current Strength	0
Fatalities	Unknown
Medal Number	57
CLASP(S)	None

MANDATE: The United Nations Mission in Liberia (UNMIL) was a peacekeeping force established in September 2003 to monitor a ceasefire agreement in Liberia following the resignation of President Charles Taylor and the conclusion of the Second Liberian Civil War. The peacekeeping mission formally withdrew on 30 March 2018. At its peak it consisted of up to 15,000 United Nations military personnel and 1,115 police officers, along with a civilian component. It superseded the United Nations Observer Mission in Liberia (UNOMIL).

BACKGROUND: The second Liberian civil war was over 20 years ago and when it ended in 2003 over a quarter of a million men, women and children were killed and hundreds of thousands civilians displaced. Much of the country's infrastructure was destroyed. The second Liberian civil war was over 20 years ago that ended in 2003 resulted in the a quarter of a million men, women and children killed and hundreds of thousands civilians. Much of the country's infrastructure was destroyed. Thousands of others were displaced internally and beyond the borders, resulting in some 850,000 refugees in neighboring countries. For most Liberians, the war was senseless. It was a form of insanity.

As the conflict wore on, the people of Liberia thought that they had been abandoned by the international community. So, the arrival of UNMIL in October 2003 with its mandate to 'support and protect' was, both timely and necessary. The peacekeepers were perceived as providers of hope, because at the time they came to Liberia, every fabric of the Liberian society was destroyed. UNMIL's contribution to Liberia has been immeasurable. It relentlessly supported every sector of the country's recovery: disarmament, demobilization and reintegration (thousands of soldiers; including child soldiers were disarmed and rehabilitated into the society); police and judicial reform (UNMIL supported the recruitment and training of officers of the Liberia National Police and the Armed Forces of Liberia);and three successful elections (2005, 2011 and 2017) which saw the peaceful transfer of power from one democratically elected government to another, the first time in more than 70 years.

The successful conduct of the 2005 elections would not have been possible without the assistance of UNMIL and this endeavor on the part of the United Nations is worth noting. The conduct of the crucial 2005 elections, the first after the total breakdown of governance, perfectly illustrates the role played by UNMIL in Liberia's recovery. It supported the National Transitional Government of Liberia (NTGL) and spearheaded the electoral process. Helicopters from UNMIL were used to move voting materials to remote areas which enabled thousands to exercise their franchise. The mission reconditioned local roads to ensure smooth travel of election workers. UNMIL's role was, however, not just limited to logistical support. It hired and trained thousands working with the National Elections Commission (NEC), including to develop election messages and provided media development training to local journalists.

The United Nations Mission in Liberia (UNMIL) deployed in 2003 to help the country rebuild, and stayed until its mandate ended in 2018 and by most accounts UNMIL was a success.

58. MINUCI - United Nations Mission in Côte d'Ivoire

MINUCIL: The ribbon has a outside stripes of United Nations blue with the colors of the The Cote D'Ivoire (Ivory Coast) flag adopted on December 3, 1959. Its design is modeled after the French Tricolore. The orange shade represents the savanna grasslands, green represents the coastal forests, while white is symbolic of the country's rivers.

Country/Location	Ivory Coast, Côte d'Ivoire
Dates	May 2003 to April 2004
Countries Participating	Austria, Bangladesh, Benin, Brazil, Gambia, Ghana, India, Ireland, Jordan, Kenya, Nepal, Niger, Nigeria, Pakistan, Paraguay, Philippines, Poland, the Republic of Moldova, Romania, Russian Federation, Senegal, Tunisia and Uruguay
Maximum Srength	75 military observers supported by 54 international civilian personnel and 55 local staff
Current Strength	0
Fatalities	None
Medal Number	58
CLASP(S)	None

MANDATE: The United Nations Mission in Côte d'Ivoire (MINUCI) was established by Security Council resolution 1479 (2003) of 13 May 2003 with a mandate to facilitate the implementation by the Ivorian parties of the Linas-Marcoussis Agreement, and including a military component complementing the operations of the French and ECOWAS forces. Basicly a politicial mission the Council approved the establishment of a small staff to support the Special Representative of the Secretary-General on political, legal, civil affairs, civilian police, elections, media and public relations, humanitarian and human rights issues, and the establishment of a military liaison group. The First Ivorian Civil War began in September 2002. In response to defense agreements with Côte d'Ivoire, dating back to independence, France deployed a military force under Opération Licorne. The Economic Community of West African States (ECOWAS) also deployed a military force the ECOWAS Mission in Côte d'Ivoire (ECOMICI). These two military forces were to serve as peacekeepers and were later tasked to keep the factions of the civil war separated while the January 2003 Linas-Marcoussis Agreement was implemented.In May 2003, the United Nations Security Council determined that the conflict in Côte d'Ivoire continued to be a threat to international peace and security and passed United Nations Security Council Resolution 1479 establishing the United Nations Mission in Côte d'Ivoire. This mission was to complement the mission of the existing French and ECOWAS forces.

BACKGROUND: The Agreement stipulated that the new Ivorian government of national reconciliation would seek assistance from ECOWAS, France and the United Nations in guaranteeing the reform and restructuring of the defence and security forces; putting in place a program for the reintegration

of all armed elements. The mission proposed the strengthening of the presence of the United Nations system in Côte d'Ivoire, in particular in the areas of security, humanitarian assistance and human rights, as well as the deployment of civilian and military observers, who would help to supervise the implementation of the Linas-Marcoussis Agreement. The Security Council endorsed the peacekeeping operation launched by ECOWAS and France, and authorized that operation to take the necessary measures to ensure the freedom of movement and security of its personnel, and to guarantee the protection of civilians facing the imminent threat of violence.

In 2004 the Security Council adopted resolution 1528, establishing the United Nations Operation in Côte d'Ivoire (UNOCI) for an initial period of 12 months. The Council also requested the Secretary-General to transfer authority from MINUCI and ECOWAS forces to UNOCI on that date, and decided to renew MINUCI's mandate until 4 April 2004. The mandate of the 6,420-strong force, in coordination with the French forces, included observing and monitoring the implementation of the comprehensive ceasefire agreement of 3 May 2003 and movements of armed groups; assistance in disarmament, demobilization, reintegration, repatriation and resettlement; protection of United Nations personnel, institutions and civilians; support for humanitarian assistance, implementation of the peace process; and assistance in the field of human rights, public information and law and order. On 4 April 2004 the MINUCI mandate ended and the UNOCI mission took over.

59. UNOCI - United Nations Mission in Côte d'Ivoire

UNOCI: The ribbon has aoutside stripes of United Nations blue with the colors of the The Cote D'Ivoire (Ivory Coast) flag adopted on December 3, 1959. Its design is modeled after the French Tricolore. The orange shade represents the savanna grasslands, green represents the coastal forests, while white is symbolic of the country's rivers. The Ivory Coast flag colors are shown in more narrow stripes than the UN-MINUCI ribbon.

Country/Location	Ivory Coast, Côte d'Ivoire
Dates	4 April 2004 to 30 June 2017
Countries Participating	Austria, Bangladesh, Benin, Brazil, France, Gambia, Ghana, India, Ireland, Jordan, Kenya, Liberia, Nepal, Niger, Nigeria, Pakistan, Paraguay, Philippines, Poland, the Republic of Moldova, Romania, Russian Federation, Senegal, Tunisia, Ukrain and Uruguay
Maximum Srength	10,954 total uniformed personnel, including 9,404 troops, 200 military observers, 1,350 police, 400 international civilian personnel, 758 local staff and 290 United Nations Volunteers.
Current Strength	0
Fatalities	144
Medal Number	59
CLASP(S)	None

MANDATE: The United Nations Operation in Côte d'Ivoire (UNOCI)(French: Opération des Nations Unies en Côte d'Ivoire, ONUCI) was a peacekeeping mission whose objective was "to facilitate the implementation by the Ivorian parties of the peace agreement signed by them in January 2003" (which aimed to end the Ivorian Civil War). The two main Ivorian parties here are the Ivorian Government forces who control the south of the country, and the New Forces (former rebels), who control the north. The UNOCI mission aimed to control a "zone of confidence" across the centre of the country separating the two parties. The mission officially ended on 30 June 2017.

BACKGROUND: UNOCI was created following a failed coup in 2002, when soldiers of the Ivorian armed forces tried to topple then-President Laurent Gbagbo.The insurgency developed into a rebellion, with rebel forces taking control of the northern half of the country. In response, both France and regional actors intervened militarily and launched a series of mediation efforts. It was in this context that the UN Security Council created UNOCI as an ambitious and full-fledged multidimensional peacekeeping operation in 2004.

In the wake of the contested 2010 presidential elections, UNOCI entered a second phase. These elections prompted a crisis that tested the mission's cooperation with French forces, the unity of the Security Council, the mission's cooperation with regional actors, and the mission's capacity to deal with a sudden deterioration in the security situation. Ultimately, UNOCI adopted a robust approach, and the crisis was resolved by force with the ouster of Gbagbo.

With the ascension of President Alassane Ouattara in 2011, UNOCI entered the third and final phase of its deployment.

During this phase it tried to support a democratically elected government that had reached power through violence.

The mission began its drawdown in 2013, and in 2017 it handed over to the UN country team with no follow-on mission in place. In the end, UNOCI was able to lift Côte d'Ivoire out of its most serious crisis since independence. It faced numerous challenges, however, and its evolution offers lessons that could be applied to other peacekeeping operations:

- *Consent of the host state*
- *Support of a permanent member of the Security Council: France influenced UNOCI in many ways: it initiated the debate in the Security Council on its creation, was the penholder on all Security Council resolutions, and deployed troops.*
- *Mandate of certification:*
- *Robust peacekeeping:*
- *Sanctions and arms embargoes*

Côted'Ivoire was elected as a nonpermanent member of the Security Council in June 2017. Its arrival to the council in January 2018 was a sign of the country's progress toward stability and sustaining peace.

60. MINUSTAH - United Nations Stabilization Mission in Haiti

MINUSTAH: The ribbon bears a band of four colours as follows: The Blue represents the United Nations. The Green symbolizes the lush green countryside and economic potential of Haiti; the Royal Blue symbolizes the ocean surrounding the island of Hispaniola ; the White symbolizes the promise of peace for the Haitian people.

Country/Location	Haiti
Dates	June, 2004 - 15 October 2017
Countries Participating	Argentina, Bolivia, Brazil, Canada, Chile, Ecuador, El Salvador, France, Guatemala, Indonesia, Jordan, Nepal, Paraguay, Peru, Philippines, Republic of Korea, Sri Lanka, United States and Uruguay. Police personnel: Argentina, Bangladesh, Benin, Brazil, Burkina Faso, Burundi, Cameroon, Canada, Central African Republic, Chad, Chile, Colombia, Côte d'Ivoire, Croatia, Egypt, El Salvador, France, Guinea, India, Indonesia, Jordan, Madagascar, Mali, Nepal, Niger, Nigeria, Norway, Pakistan, Philippines, Romania, Russian Federation, Rwanda, Senegal, Serbia, Sierra Leone, Spain, Sri Lanka, Sweden, Togo, Turkey, United States, Uruguay and Yemen.
Maximum Srength	28 February 2013) 6,685 troops and 2,607 police
Current Strength	0
Fatalities	175
Medal Number	60
CLASP(S)	None

MANDATE: The United Nations Stabilization Mission in Haiti (MINUSTAH) was established on 1 June 2004 by Security Council resolution 1542. The UN mission succeeded a Multinational Interim Force (MIF) authorized by the Security Council in February 2004 after President Bertrand Aristide departed Haiti for exile in the aftermath of an armed conflict which spread to several cities across the country.

BACKGROUND: The devastating earthquake, which resulted in more than 220,000 deaths (according to Haitian Government figures) delivered a severe blow to country's already shaky economy and infrastructure. The Security Council, by resolution 1908 of 19 January 2010, endorsed the Secretary-General's recommendation to increase the overall force levels of MINUSTAH to support the immediate recovery, reconstruction and stability efforts in the country. MINUSTAH would concentrate on assisting the Haitian National Police in providing security within the country after the earthquake, while American and Canadian military forces distributed humanitarian aid and provide security for aid distribution.

The Mission mobilizeed its logistical resources to assist in the effort to contain and treat the cholera outbreak of October 2010. Many Haitians blamed the cholera on raw sewage from a Napal UN unit draining into a major river used as a water supply. Other charges of excessive force and sexual misconduct by UN troops and police have created bitterness by some Haitians.

Following the completion of Presidential elections in 2011, MINUSTAH worked to fulfil its original mandate to restore a secure and stable environment, to promote the political process, to strengthen Haiti's Government institutions and rule-of-law-structures, as well as to promote and to protect human rights. The security situation in Haiti has vastly improved since the Mission's

establishment in 2004: kidnappings are down by over 95% and rates of homicides are among the lowest since 2013. MINUSTAH helped the Police Nationale d'Haiti to restore control of many neighborhoods in Port-au-Prince once controlled by gangs.

Hurricane Matthew in 2016 was another major blow to the people of Haiti and the UN and other countries provided humanitarian aid to help stablize the country. Over its 13 years of service, the UN Mission has funded more than 2,250 projects, valued at more than $125 million, and spent over seven billion dollars to help stabilize the country.

In April 2017, the Council decided in resolution 2350 (2017) that the UN Stabilization Mission in Haiti (MINUSTAH) would close on 15 October 2017, transitioning to a smaller follow-up peacekeeping Mission which would support Government efforts to strengthen rule-of-law institutions, further develop the Haitian National Police and engage in human rights monitoring, reporting and analysis.

Philippine troops were popular among the Haitians. UN Photo

61. ONUB - United Nations Operation in Burundi

ONUB: The ribbon has an outside stripes of United Nations blue with the colors of the the Burundi flag adopted on June 28, 1967. The red in the flag stands for the independence struggle, the green for hope and the white for peace.

Country/Location	Burundi
Dates	1 June 2004 to 31 December 2006
Countries Participating	Algeria, Bangladesh, Belgium, Benin, Bolivia, Burkina Faso, Chad, China, Egypt, Ethiopia, Gabon, Gambia, Ghana, Guatemala, Guinea, India, Jordan, Kenya, Kyrgyzstan, Malawi, Malaysia, Mali, Mozambique, Namibia, Nepal, Netherlands, Niger, Nigeria, Pakistan, Paraguay, Peru, Philippines, Portugal, Republic of Korea, Romania, Russia, Senegal, Serbia and Montenegro, South Africa, Spain, Sri Lanka, Thailand, Togo, Tunisia, Uruguay, Yemen and Zambia.
Maximum Srength	5,665 total uniformed personnel, including 5,400 troops, 168 military observers and 97 police; supported by 316 international civilian personnel and 383 local civilian staff and 156 United Nations Volunteers
Current Strength	0
Fatalities	21 military personnel, 1 police, 1 international civilian personnel, 1 local civilian personnel
Medal Number	61
CLASP(S)	None

MANDATE: Having determined that the situation in Burundi continued to constitute a threat to international peace and security in the region and acting under Chapter VII of the UN Charter, the Security Council, by its resolution 1545 of 21 May 2004, decided to establish the United Nations Operation in Burundi (ONUB) in order to support and help to implement the efforts undertaken by Burundians to restore lasting peace and bring about national reconciliation, as provided under the Arusha Agreement.

BACKGROUND: The African Union, and later the United Nations, each deployed a peacekeeping mission in Burundi in the early 2000s to facilitate and later maintain the tenuous peace brokered by international negotiating teams between the many parties involved in the 12-year (1993-2005) 18-belligerent civil war. The United Nations Operation in Burundi (ONUB) was established to support the efforts undertaken by Burundians to restore lasting peace and bring about national reconciliation, as provided under the Agreement on Peace and Reconciliation in Burundi, signed in Arusha, Tanzania, which meant to end a decade-long, ethnically-based civil war between the Tutsi minority and the Hutu majority.

During its two-and-half-year presence in Burundi, ONUB completed its mandated tasks including assisting disarmament, demobilization, rehabilitation and reintegration of ex-combatants; supporting elections which resulted in new democratic institutions at the communal, local and national level; monitoring ceasefire agreements; and promoting human rights, rule of law, economic development and social justice.

ONUB played a key supportive role in the implementation of the national DDR programme since it was launched in December 2004. ONUB also provided security to ex-combatants at the demobilization centres. As of December 2006, a total of 21,769 ex-combatants including 3,015 children and 494 women were demobilized. The United Nations was in charge of supporting the reform of the Burundian police force. A total of 2,445 police officers benefited from ONUB expertise. In addition to its traditional training activities, ONUB also worked with international donors to acquire equipment for the poorly-equipped security structure. The now 20,000-strong new National Burundian Force is fully integrated, active and present all over the country.

ONUB supported the National Independent Election Commission (CENI) to achieve the daunting task of organizing an eight-month long electoral process, which involved six separate elections.

The UN leadership on the ground was much more aggressive in controling sexual abuse scandals such as were occuring in the Congo. Logistics were a serious problem especially for South African troops as was the task of keeping an appearance of neutrality when working with the government. However on the whole both African nations and the UN considered the mission to have been successful with a host of lessons learned for the future.

Pakistan troops prepare for movement. UN Photo

62. UNMIS - United Nations Mission in the Sudan

UNMIS: *The ribbon has two outer bands of UN blue, representing the UN presence in the Sudan. Inside the two bands, there are alternating stripes of UN Blue and White. The ribbon is United Nations blue with three thin stripes of royal blue in the centre separated by two thin white stripes.*

Country/Location	Sudan
Dates	24 March 2005 – 9 July 2011
Countries Participating	Military personnel: Australia, Bangladesh, Belgium, Benin, Bolivia, Brazil, Burkina Faso, Cambodia, Canada, China, Croatia, Denmark, Ecuador, Egypt, El Salvador, Fiji, Finland, Germany, Ghana, Greece, Guatemala, Guinea, India, Indonesia, Japan, Jordan, Kenya, Kyrgystan, Malaysia, Mali, Moldova, Mongolia, Namibia, Nepal, Netherlands, New Zealand, Nigeria, Norway, Pakistan, Paraguay, Peru, Philippines, Poland, Republic of Korea, Romania, Russian Federation, Rwanda, Sierra Leone, Sri Lanka, Sweden, Switzerland, Tanzania, Thailand, Turkey, Uganda, Ukraine, United Kingdom, Yemen and Zambia.
	Police personnel: Argentina, Australia, Bangladesh, Bosnia and Herzegovina, Brazil, Canada, China, Egypt, El Salvador, Ethiopia, Fiji, Gambia, Germany, Ghana, India, Indonesia, Jamaica, Jordan, Kenya, Kyrgystan, Malaysia, Mali, Namibia, Nepal, Netherlands, Nigeria, Norway, Pakistan, Philippines, Russian Federation, Rwanda, Samoa, Sri Lanka, Sweden, Turkey, Uganda, Ukraine, United States, Yemen, Zambia and Zimbabwe.:
Maximum Srength	(31 January 2011) 10,519 total uniformed personnel, including 9,304 troops, 513 military observers, 702 police officers, 966 international civilian personnel, 2,837 local civilian staff, 477 United Nations Volunteers
Current Strength	0
Fatalities	23 troops, 3 police, 3 military observers, 8 international civilians, 22 local civilians, 1 other
Medal Number	62
CLASP(S)	None

MANDATE: On 24 March 2005, the Security Council by resolution 1590 (2005) established the United Nations Mission in the Sudan (UNMIS). The tasks of UNMIS, among others, was: to support implementation of the Comprehensive Peace Agreement; to facilitate and coordinate, within its capabilities and in its areas of deployment, the voluntary return of refugees and internally displaced persons and humanitarian assistance; to assist the parties in the mine action sector; to contribute towards international efforts to protect and promote human rights in the Sudan.

BACKGROUND: The Ceasefire Agreement came into effect on the date of signature of the Comprehensive Peace Agreement (CPA). Not all belligerent groups had been party to the peace negotiations and many proclaimed their displeasure that they had not been directly involved or their interests taken into account and stated they will not automatically feel bound by the CPA as negotiated by government of Sudan and SPLM/A. There was also an increase of well armed criminal elements that could see the UN as a lucrative target, including groups operating cross border such as the Lord's Resistance Army.

UNMIS was not intially able to deploy to Darfur due to the Government of the Sudan's steadfast opposition to a peacekeeping operation undertaken solely by the United Nations. Following prolonged and intensive negotiations and significant international pressure, the Sudan Government accepted peacekeeping operation in Darfur. On 31 July, 2006 the Security Council, authorized the establishment of the United Nations-African Union Hybrid Operation in Darfur (UNAMID).

For its part, UNMIS supported implementation of the 2005 Comprehensive Peace Agreement, by providing political support to the parties, monitoring and verifying security arrangements and offering assistance, including governance, recovery and development. The Mission focused on the parties' commitments, including the redeployment of forces, a resolution over the oil-rich Abyei region, and national elections in 2010 and the referendums in 2011.

The referendum for Southern Sudan was held on schedule in January 2011, with, 98.83% of participants, voting for independence. The peaceful and credible conduct of the referendum was a great achievement for all Sudanese as well as the Comprehensive Peace Agreement (CPA) partners, the Government of Sudan and the Government of Southern Sudan kept their commitment to maintain peace and stability throughout this crucial period.

63. UNMIT - United Nations Mission in Timor

Country/Location	Timor-Leste
Dates	25 August 2006 – 31 December 2012
Countries Participating	Military liaison and staff officers: Australia, Bangladesh, Brazil, China, Fiji, Japan, India, Malaysia, Nepal, New Zealand, Pakistan, Philippines, Portugal, Sierra Leone, Singapore.
	Police personnel: Australia, Bangladesh, Brazil, Canada, China, Croatia, Egypt, El Salvador, Egypt, Fiji, Gambia, India, Jamaica, Japan, Jordan, Kyrgyzstan, Malaysia, Namibia, Nepal, New Zealand, Nigeria, Pakistan, Palau, Philippines, Portugal, Republic of Korea, Romania, Russian Federation, Samoa, Senegal, Singapore, South Korea, Spain, Sri Lanka, Sweden, Thailand, Turkey, Uganda, Ukraine, Uruguay, United States, Vanuatu, Yemen, Zambia, and Zimbabwe.
Maximum Srength	1,608 police personnel, 34 military liaison and staff officers, and an appropriate civilian component
Current Strength	0
Fatalities	9 police, 4 local civilians, 4 international civilian
Medal Number	63
CLASP(S)	None

UNMIT: The ribbon is United Nations blue with a central red stripe flanked with thin stripes of yellow, black and white. These colors represent The new East Timor flag officially adopted in 2002. The yellow represents its prior colonial history, the black represents the prior obscurantism, while red is symbolic of the struggle for liberation, and the white is symbolic of peace.

MANDATE: The United Nations Integrated Mission in East Timor (UNMIT) objectives were "to support the Government in consolidating stability, enhancing a culture of democratic governance, and facilitating political dialogue among Timorese stakeholders to bring about a process of national reconciliation and to foster social cohesion. The multidimensional, integrated UN peacekeeping operatio was established by Security Council resolution in the wake of a major political, humanitarian and security crisis which erupted in Timor-Leste in April-May 2006. The crisis displaced up to 150,000 people, who took shelter in camps throughout the capital city, Dili, and Baucau.

BACKGROUND: UNMIT provided interim law enforcement and public security until Timor-Leste's national police could be reconstituted. The broad mandate included helping the Government organize elections; build capacity in governance, justice and security sectors; strengthen human rights mechanisms; and complete investigations into cases of serious human rights violations committed in 1999. The mandate provided support for the Government's mechanisms for donor coordination and for promoting gender equality in building institutions and making policy.

In September 2011, the Government and UNMIT signed a Joint Transition Plan (JTP) to guide planning for UNMIT's expected withdrawal by 2012. The plan, the first of its kind in peacekeeping, identified 129 UNMIT activities to be completed by the end of 2012 or handed over to partners. Each year, UNMIT's mandate translated into a 1600-member United Nations police

component and a number of military liaison officers, as well as hundreds of Timorese, international and volunteer civilian personnel. Since UNMIT's creation, its personnel worked with all segments of Timorese society, from the police and armed forces, to the National Parliament and political parties, and to civil society groups and news media throughout the country, to help Timor-Leste achieve stability, build a resilient state, and improve the lives of all its citizens.

Thanks to the resilience and determination of the Timorese people and their leaders, and with the support of the international community, Timor-Leste has made tremendous progress since 2006. The displaced people have peacefully returned to their homes. Since March 2011, the national police have been responsible for policing throughout the country, with no major breakdown of law and order. Timorese news media and civil society have grown stronger, making important contributions to the democratic debate in the country. Poverty is decreasing as a result of public investments in infrastructure and services, fueled by the income from Timor-Leste's petroleum resources, which are managed through the Petroleum Fund. Since 2005, life expectancy at birth increased by more than two years and now averages 62.1 years. Primary school enrolment, a key element to future stability and growth, jumped from 63 per cent in 2006 to 90 per cent today and the country is on track to eradicate adult illiteracy. 2012 saw free and peaceful presidential and parliamentary elections, followed by the smooth formation of a new Government. UNMIT troops left the country at the end of 2012.

64. UNAMID - United Nations Hybrid Operation in Darfur

UNAMID: The ribbon is United Nations blue with a central white stripe flanked by stripes of yellow-gold and green. The blue and white are the UN colours while the gold and green represent the African Union. The Sudan is represented by green and white, with white also the symbol of peace.

Country/Location	Darfur, Sudan
Dates	2007-2020
Countries Participating	Troop contributing countries: Ethiopia, Rwanda, Pakistan, Egypt, Tanzania, Indonesia, China, Nepal, Bangladesh, Gambia, Nigeria, Kenya and Senegal.
	Other contributors of military personnel: Ecuador, Germany, Ghana, Iran, Jordan, South Korea, Malaysia, Namibia, Peru, Sierra Leone, South Africa, Thailand, Togo, Zambia, Bhutan, Cambodia, Malawi, Magnolia and Zimbabwe.
	Contributors of police personnel: Jordan, Malawi, Rwanda, Namibia, Tunisia, Nepal, Ghana, Sierra Leone, Bangladesh, Zambia, Burkina Faso, Cameron, Egypt, Ethiopia, Gambia, Germany, Djibouti, Indonesia, Kyrgyzstan, Madagascar, Togo, Brazil, Nigeria, Pakistan, Senegal, Tanzania, Zimbabwe, Bhutan, Fiji, Magnolia, Turkey, Tajikistan, Samoa and Thailand.
Maximum Srength	19,555 Military personnel, 3,772 Police, 2620 Civilians
Current Strength	0
Fatalities	276
Medal Number	64
CLASP(S)	None

MANDATE: The African Union-United Nations Hybrid Operation in Darfur (UNAMID) is a joint African Union (AU) and United Nations (UN) peacekeeping mission formally approved by United Nations Security Council Resolution 1769 on 31 July 2007, to bring stability to the war-torn Darfur region of Sudan while peace talks on a final settlement continue. UNAMID has the protection of civilians as its core mandate, but is also tasked with contributing to security for humanitarian assistance, monitoring and verifying implementation of agreements, assisting an inclusive political process, contributing to the promotion of human rights and the rule of law, and monitoring and reporting on the situation along the borders with Chad and the Central African Republic (CAR).

BACKGROUND: The western Sudanese region of Darfur has been plagued by a war between Sudanese government forces and the indigenous population since 2003. UNAMID was established by the Security Council in July 2007 to help maintain and mediate peace. On 29 June 2017 Resolution 2363 was adopted by the Security Council which, in addition to renewing the mission's mandate, decided to draw down UNAMID's troop and police strength over the next year in two phases, while closely monitoring the situation on the ground.

However, the Security Council adopted a resolution to extend the mandate of the UN-African Union Hybrid Operation in Darfur (UNAMID) for a year, till Oct. 31, 2020. Resolution 2495, calls on the Sudanese government, Darfur armed movements, and all other stakeholders to strive for peace to allow for UNAMID's exit. The resolution decided that till March 31, 2020, UNAMID shall maintain its current troop and police ceilings, and that during this period, UNAMID will maintain all team sites for mandate implementation, except its sector headquarters in South Darfur.

The planned drawdown and exit of UNAMID was delayed by a series of events in Sudan that resulted in the ouster of longtime leader Omar al-Bashir in April 2019, followed by months of unrest. The Security Council had to approve a four-month technical roll-over of UNAMID's mandate in June 2019 amid a stalemate of Sudan's political situation, and put on hold the mission's drawdown.

The Security Council intended to decide by March 31, 2020, courses of action regarding the drawdown and exit of UNAMID, and to adopt a new resolution at the same time on a follow-on presence to UNAMID.

The resolution decided that UNAMID shall focus on support to the peace process in Darfur; support to peacebuilding activities; the protection of civilians, monitoring and reporting on human rights, the facilitation of humanitarian assistance and the safety and security of humanitarian personnel, and contribute to the creation of the necessary security conditions for the voluntary, informed, safe, dignified and sustainable return of refugees and internally displaced people, or, where appropriate, their local integration or relocation to a third location.

The outbreak of COVID 19 in Darfur saw UNAMID provided Personnel Protection Equipment (PPE) to the Ministry of Health and Social Development's first COVID-19 Isolation Centre established in Zalingei, central Darfur.

65. MINURCAT- United Nations Mission in the Central African Republic and Chad

MINURCAT: The ribbon is United Nations blue with five stripes representing the colors of the flags of Chad and the CAR. The blue-yellow-red colours of Chad are a combination of the blue-white-red of France, the former colonial power, and the green-yellow-red of the Pan-African (e.g., Ethiopian) ones. Central African Republic colors are blue-white-yellow-green and red.

Country/Location	Central African Republic and Chad
Dates	25 September 2007 – 31 December 2010
Countries Participating	Military personnel: Austria, Albania, Bangladesh, Bolivia, Brazil, Benin, Burkina Faso, Croatia, Cambodia, Democratic Republic of the Congo, Denmark, Ecuador, Ethiopia, Egypt, France, Finland, Gabon, Gambia, Ghana, Italy, Ireland, Jordan, Kenya, Kyrgyzstan, Mongolia, Malawi, Mali, Norway, Nepal, Nigeria, Namibia, Poland, Pakistan, Paraguay, Portugal, Russian Federation, Rwanda, Sri Lanka, Serbia, Senegal, Spain, Togo, Tunisia, Uganda, United States, Uruguay, Yemen and Zambia.
	Police personnel: Benin, Burkina Faso, Burundi, Cameroon, Côte d'Ivoire, Egypt, Finland, France, Guinea, Jordan, Libya, Madagascar, Mali, Niger, Portugal, Rwanda, Senegal, Sweden, Togo, Turkey and Yemen.
Maximum Strength	5,200 military personnel and 27 military liaison officers, 300 police officers
Current Strength	0
Fatalities	2 troop, 1 international civilian, 5 local civilian
Medal Number	65
CLASP(S)	None

MANDATE: The United Nations Mission in the Central African Republic and Chad (MINURCAT) was a peacekeeping mission established by the Security Council on September 25, 2007 to provide a multidimensional presence of up to 350 police and military personnel to eastern Chad and north-eastern Central African Republic.

BACKGROUND: The mission came as a response to the dire situation of an estimated 230,000 refugees from Darfur who continued to flee into bordering eastern Chad and north-eastern Central African Republic (CAR). Armed Sudanese rebel groups had continuously carried out attacks across the Sudanese border, endangering local residents and Darfurian refugees alike.

The mission followed on from a resolution in July 2007 sending UNAMID into the region and a resolution in August 2006 sending UNMIS there. The Secretary-General drafted a report outlining the shape of the mission he thought should be sent there and received assurance from the European Union of its contribution of troops.

Although the EUFOR forces were originally scheduled to deploy in November 2007, they was delayed until February due to a lack of equipment. The mission reached its Initial Operational Capability on 15 March 2008 and was replaced by UN forces under the same MINURCAT mandate on 15 March 2009. A later resolution to the MINURCAT mandate, Security Council Resolution 1913, extended the stationing of the mission until 15 May 2010 allowing further discussions with the Chadian government which asked for the mandate not be renewed. A further extension was done until the end of 2010.

The Mission completed its mandate on 31 December 2010, in accordance with Security Council resolution 1923 and at the request of the Chadian Government, which had pledged full responsibility for protecting civilians on its territory.

Following MINURCAT's withdrawal, the UN country team and the UN Integrated Peacebuilding Office in the Central African Republic (BINUCA) remained in the country to continue to work for the benefit of the Chadian people.

Reporting to the Security Council in December, the Secretary-General said "MINURCAT has been an unusual and unique United Nations peacekeeping operation in that it was devoted solely to contributing to the protection of civilians, without an explicit political mandate. It has gone through the stages of planning, deployment and withdrawal in the short span of less than four years while enduring adversities in each year.

Peacekeeper with Sudanese refugee children in Bahai, Eastern Chad. UN Photo

66. MONUSCO - UNITED NATIONS ORGANIZATION STABILIZATION MISSION IN THE D.R. of the CONGO

MONUSCO: The medal was established on 2 May 2000. The ribbon has two outer bands of UN blue, representing the UN presence in the Democratic Republic of Congo (DRC). Inside the two bands, there are two equal bars in yellow, they represent the dawn of peace and prosperity. The dark blue in the middle of the yellow represents the Conge river.

Country/Location	Democratic Republic of the Congo
Dates	2010-PRESENT
Countries Participating	Military personnel: Bangladesh, Belgium, Benin, Bolivia, Bosnia and Herzegovina, Brazil, Burkina Faso, Cameroon, Canada, China, Côte d'Ivoire, Czech Republic, Egypt, France, Ghana, Guatemala, India, Indonesia, Ireland, Jordan, Kenya, Malawi, Malaysia, Mali, Mongolia, Morocco, Nepal, Niger, Nigeria, Pakistan, Paraguay, Peru, Poland, Romania, Russian Federation, Senegal, Serbia, South Africa, Sri Lanka, Sweden, Switzerland, Tunisia, Ukraine, United Kingdom, United Republic of Tanzania, United States, Uruguay, Yemen and Zambia. In addition, the following nations have contributed with police personnel: Bangladesh, Benin, Brazil, Burkina Faso, Cameroon, Chad, Egypt, France, Ghana, Guinea, Jordan, Madagascar, Mali, Niger, Nigeria, Romania, Senegal, Sweden, Switzerland,, Russian Federation, Togo, Tunisia, Turkey, Ukraine and Yemen
Maximum Srength	16,215 Military, 1,441police, 3200 civilans
Current Strength	0
Fatalities	182
Medal Number	66
CLASP(S)	None

MANDATE: MONUSCO took over from an earlier UN peacekeeping operation – the United Nations Organization Mission in Democratic Republic of the Congo (MONUC) – on 1 July 2010. It was done in accordance with Security Council resolution 1925 of 28 May to reflect the new phase reached in the country. The new mission has been authorized to use all necessary means to carry out its mandate relating, among other things, to the protection of civilians, humanitarian personnel and human rights defenders under imminent threat of physical violence and to support the Government of the DRC in its stabilization and peace consolidation efforts.

BACKGROUND: The mission was established to protect civilians from violence, facilitate humanitarian access, and disarm, demobilize, and reintegrate former combatants back into society. The Security Council has altered the mandate in the following years, including creating a "Force Intervention Brigade," the first of its kind for a UN peacekeeping mission, which carries out targeted offensive operations to neutralize and disarm armed groups in Eastern Congo where high levels of insecurity and criminality persist in different regions of the DRC. In the provinces of North Kivu, South Kivu, and Ituri,there where open clashes between government forces and a wide array of nonstate armed groups. Some estimated 130 armed groups were operating in the country are deeply connected to local communities.

Attacks and volience continued through 2012 and in March 2013, the United Nations Security Council authorized the deployment of an intervention brigade within MONUSCO to carry out targeted offensive operations, with or without the Congolese national army, against armed groups that threaten peace in eastern DRC. The March 23 Movement was given a 48-hour ultimatum by the UN to leave Goma area or face "use of force." Between 21 and 29 August, heavy fighting outside Goma left 57 rebels, 10–23 government soldiers, 14 civilians and one Tanzanian U.N. peacekeeper dead. 720 government soldiers and 10 U.N. peacekeepers were also wounded. After the 2014 South Kivu attack in June 2014, the UN announced it would send MONUSCO peacekeeping troops to the area to protect the population.

A major area in which the peacekeeping mission has had an impact is its contribution towards reunification of the country. A second area of major impact is the preventing of a major reoccurrence of violent conflicts. The mission also provided services and stimulated the local economy and in many cases the development of vital infrastructure such as airports, access roads river traffic and telecommunications. It has had a major impact on contributing to the democratic process in developing an occasionally impartial media. Unfortunately the main constraint on this mission has been the decreasing degree of cooperation by the host state in the past years. Quite often the mission had to work with a government that did not want it to be there. It has been a long-term investment by the United Nations with a number of positive effects but the final results are still uncertain.

67. UNISFA -The United Nations Interim Security Force for Abyei

USISFA: The ribbon is United Nations blue with five stripes representing the colors of the surrounding countries. White stripes represent hope and he green-yellow-black of the Pan-African (e.g., Ethiopian) and Sudan.

Country/Location	Abyei, Sudan and South Sudan
Dates	June -2011 to present
Countries Participating	UNISFA is almost entirely composed of personnel from neighboring Ethiopia, based on a 2011 agreement between Sudan and South Sudan to demilitarize the area and allow Ethiopian monitors. Indivdual staff and experts from a host of countries.
Maximum Srength	5,326 military personnel, 650 police personnel and appropriate civilian support
Current Strength	3489 troops, 27 Police, 2217 Civilians,140 Experts on mission, 116 Staff Officers, 32 Volunteers
Fatalities	36
Medal Number	67
CLASP(S)	None

MANDATE: The Security Council, by its resolution 1990 of 27 June 2011, responded to the urgent situation in Sudan's Abyei region by establishing the United Nations Interim Security Force for Abyei (UNISFA). The Security Council was deeply concerned by the violence, escalating tensions and population displacement.

The operation has been tasked with monitoring the flashpoint border between north and south and facilitating the delivery of humanitarian aid, and is authorized to use force in protecting civilians and humanitarian workers in Abyei.

BACKGROUND: UNISFA's establishment came after the Government of Sudan and the Sudan People's Liberation Movement (SPLM) reached an agreement in Addis Ababa, Ethiopia, to demilitarize Abyei and let Ethiopian troops monitor the area.

UNISFA is almost entirely composed of personnel from neighboring Ethiopia, based on a 2011 agreement between Sudan and South Sudan to demilitarize the area and allow Ethiopian monitors. UNISFA was authorized by the U.N. Security Council on the eve of South Sudan's independence in June 2011, in an effort to mitigate direct conflict between Sudan and South Sudan at a prominent disputed area on their border. The mission's mandate originally focused only on Abyei a contested border territory and historic flashpoint for conflict that was accorded special semiautonomous status in the 2005 Comprehensive Peace Agreement (CPA) between Sudan's government and southern rebels. The mandate was expanded in late 2011 to support broader border security arrangements between the two countries, including a Joint Border Verification and Monitoring Mechanism (JBVMM), which the CPA signatories agreed to

establish to monitor the full Sudan-South Sudan border. UNISFA's deployment to Abyei defused a violent standoff between the two countries' militaries, but tensions among local communities still have the potential to destabilize the border. Under the CPA, the residents of Abyei were to vote in a referendum in 2011 on whether the area should retain its special status in Sudan or join South Sudan, but an officially sanctioned process has yet to occur. The final status of Abyei is likely to remain unresolved until Sudan and South Sudan negotiate a solution. The April 2019 ouster of Sudan's President Omar al Bashir and the unfolding political transition may affect the situation in Abyei and other border areas.

When Sudanese troops and allied militia seized Abyei after its referendum was postponed, the Obama Administration declared the move to be an invasion of area and thus a violation of the CPA. The Security Council similarly condemned Sudan's "taking of military control" of Abyei home to the Ngok Dinka, a subgroup of South Sudan's largest ethnic group. The Ngok constitute a majority of the area's permanent residents. The Misseriya, a pastoralist Arab tribe, have historically used the area seasonally, but some have settled, and the Government of Sudan has sought to elevate their position in determining Abyei's future.

U.N. Security Council Resolution authorized UNISFA. Sudan's army subsequently withdrew as UNISFA deployed, and the mission's presence has since been seen as a deterrent to conflict between the two countries' forces. While relations between Sudan and South Sudan have improved in recent years, the instability in South Sudan and Sudan's Southern Kordofan state poses risks, and the political transition in Sudan creates further uncertainty regarding stability in the region.

68. UNMISS - UNITED NATIONS MISSION IN SOUTH SUDAN

UNMISS: *The ribbon has two United Nations blue stripes on the edges, followed by two white stripes and one green central stripe. Four black lines separate each of these stripes.*

Country/Location	South Sudan
Dates	2011 to Present
Countries Participating	India has supplied 2,237 troops; Other contributors of troops are Australia,[18] Bangladesh, Belarus, Benin, Bolivia, Brazil, Cambodia, Canada, China, Colombia, Denmark, Dominican Republic, Egypt, El Salvador, Fiji, Germany, Ghana, Guatemala, Guinea, India, Indonesia, Japan, Jordan, Kenya, Kyrgyzstan, Mali, Mongolia, Namibia, Nepal, Netherlands, New Zealand, Nigeria, Norway, Oman, Papua New Guinea, Paraguay, Peru, Poland, Republic of Korea, Romania, Russian Federation, Rwanda, Senegal, Sri Lanka, Sweden, Switzerland, Timor-Leste, Togo, Uganda, Ukraine, United Kingdom, United Republic of Tanzania, United States, Vietnam, Yemen, Zambia and Zimbabwe.
	Police contributed by Algeria, Argentina, Bangladesh, Bosnia and Herzegovina, Brazil, Canada, China, El Salvador, Ethiopia, Fiji, Finland, Gambia, Germany, Ghana, India, Kenya, Kyrgyzstan, Malaysia, Namibia, Nepal, Netherlands, Nigeria, Norway, Oman, Panama, Philippines, Russian Federation, Rwanda, Samoa, Senegal, Sierra Leone, South Africa, Sri Lanka, Sweden, Switzerland, Thailand, Turkey, Uganda, Ukraine, United States, Zambia and Zimbabwe
Maximum Srength	17,000 troops, including 4,000 for the Regional Protection Force, 2,101 police personnel
Current Strength	---
Fatalities	72
Medal Number	68
CLASP(S)	None

MANDATE: UNMISS was established on July 9, 2011, the date of South Sudan's independence from Sudan. It replaced the U.N. Mission in Sudan (UNMIS), which had supported implementation of the peace deal that ended Sudan's north-south civil war. UNMISS, currently authorized through March 2020, is currently the U.N.'s second largest peacekeeping mission.

BACKGROUND: UNMISS was established with the aim of consolidating peace and security in the world's newest country, and helping to establish conditions for development after decades of war. The outbreak of a new internal conflict in December 2013, however, fundamentally changed the mission and its relationship with the host government. The war, now in its sixth year, has displaced more than 4 million people, and by some estimates over 380,000 people have been killed, including at least 190,000 in violent deaths.

Shortly after the fighting began, the U.N. Security Council authorized an expansion of the mission As a result, the mandate changed from one that had supported peace-building, state-building, and the extension of state authority to one that sought strict impartiality in relations with both sides of the conflict, while pursuing

four key tasks under a Chapter VII mandate: protecting civilians, monitoring and investigating human rights abuses, facilitating conditions conducive to aid delivery, and supporting a ceasefire monitoring.

In September 2018, South Sudan's two largest warring factions—those of President Salva Kiir and his rival, Riek Machar—signed a new peace deal. Experts debate whether the deal is a viable framework for sustainable peace. The International Crisis Group (ICG) contends that, at minimum, "it is not a finished product and requires revision, a reality that mediators are not yet ready to admit." Implementation of the agreement is significantly behind schedule. The planned formation of a new unity government, delayed from May to November 2019, is in question as concerns about the accord's security arrangements remain unaddressed. The 2018 ceasefire has reduced the fighting in most parts of the country, but clashes continue in some areas, and U.N. reports continued use of conflict-related sexual violence by the warring parties and targeted" attacks on civilians, notably those perceived to be associated with opposition groups. There is mounting concerns that this latest deal could collapse.

69. UNSMIS - United Nations Supervision Mission in Syria

UNSMIS: The ribbon has two United Nations blue stripes on the edges, followed by alternating white and green white stripes and one red central stripe.the green and white stripes represent hope in bring peace to the civil war in Syria.

Country/Location	Syria
Dates	April 2012 – August 2012
Countries Participating	Armenia, Bangladesh, Benin, Brazil, Burkina Faso, Burundi, Cambodia, Chad, China, Croatia, Czech Republic, Denmark, Ecuador, Egypt, Fiji, Finland, France, Ghana, Indonesia, Ireland, Italy, Jordan, Kenya, Kyrgyzstan, Mauritania, Morocco, Nepal, Netherlands, New Zealand, Niger, Nigeria, Norway, Paraguay, Philippines, Romania, Russian Federation, Senegal, Slovenia, Switzerland, Togo, Yemen and Zimbabwe.
Maximum Srength	278 military observers, 81 international civilian staff, 40 local civilian staff
Current Strength	0
Fatalities	1 (local civilian)
Medal Number	69
CLASP(S)	None

MANDATE: The United Nations Supervision Mission in Syria (UNSMIS) was established by Security Council resolution of 21 April 2012 as part of the Joint Special Envoy's six-point plan designed to end the escalating conflict. One of the key elements of the plan was to bring about a sustained cessation of armed violence in all its forms by all parties with an effective UN supervision mechanism.

BACKGROUND: With a record rapid deployment, UNSMIS was fully operational on 30 May. As at 30 June, UNSMIS had 278 military observers at its Damascus headquarters and eight team sites, in Aleppo, Damascus, Deir-ez-Zor, Hama, Homs, Idlib, Deraa and Tartus, and 121 civilian staff addressing political and civil affairs and human rights matters, administration and support at Mission headquarters, with mixed military-civilian teams at five of the sites.

UNSMIS operations focused in and around population centres, in relation to both military monitoring and civilian interactions. To consolidate the cessation of violence, saturated patrolling was conducted in those areas. From 16 April until early May, hostilities in Syria were characterized by low-intensity fighting and a general reduction in violence. The cessation of violence established under the six-point plan and the presence of UNSMIS seemed to have a dampening effect in the areas where observers were deployed. The Mission worked actively in support of all aspects of the plan, and the observers, by establishing facts, contributed to building the international consensus.

However the agreed cessation of violence held only briefly. The second week of May saw a return to unrestrained and increasing hostilities, which by mid-June had reached or even surpassed pre-12 April levels. Government forces appeared to be engaged in a major coordinated effort to reclaim urban centres hitherto under opposition control, increasingly directed at larger towns, using a combination of helicopters, armored units, artillery, and infantry, supplemented by militia forces. The levels of violence ultimately rendered UNSMIS' own mandate implementation activities untenable. On 15 June, the Mission suspended its normal operations in light of the violence, obstacles to monitoring access, and direct targeting of its personnel and assets.

UNSMIS was extended for a final period of 30 days. According to resolution S/RES/2059, the Council would only consider further extensions to the mission "in the event that the Security Council confirmed the cessation of the use of heavy weapons and a reduction in the level of violence sufficient by all sides" to allow the UNSMIS monitors to implement their mandate. The two conditions set by the Council were not met. UNSMIS mandate came to an end at midnight on 19 August 2012.

United Nations observers inspecting a residential area with Free Syrian Army gunmen at Talbisah area in Homs city. UN Photo

70. MINUSMA - U.N. Multidimensional Integrated Stabilization Mission in Mali

MINUSMA: The ribbon is United Nations blue with a wide central royal blue stripe flanked on the left with thin stripes of green, gold, and red, representing Mali's national colours, and on the right with a stripe of buff color.

Country/Location	Mali
Dates	April 2013 - Present
Countries Participating	Algeria, Austria, Bangladesh, Belgium, Benin, Bosnia and Herzegovina, Burkina, Faso, Canada, Chad, China, Ivory Coast, Czech Republic, Denmark, Dominican Republic, Egypt, El Salvado,r Estonia, Finland, France, Gambia, Germany, Ghana, Guinea, Guinea-Bissau, Ireland, Italy, Jordan, Kenya, Latvia, Liberia, Lithuania, Mauritania, Nepal, Netherlands, Niger, Nigeria, Norway,Oman, Pakistan, Portugal, Romania, Rwanda, Senegal, Sierra Leone, Sri Lanka, Sweden, Switzerland, Tanzania, Togo, Tunisia, United Kingdom, United States
Maximum Srength	13,300 military personnel, 2,000 Police, Appropiate civilian component
Current Strength	15,441
Fatalities	208
Medal Number	70
CLASP(S)	None

MANDATE: The Security Council established the U.N. Multidimensional Integrated Stabilization Mission in Mali (MINUSMA) in 2013 after state institutions collapsed in the face of an ethnic separatist rebellion in the north, a military coup, and an Islamist insurgent takeover of the north of the country.

BACKGROUND: The mission absorbed a short-lived African intervention force and U.N. political mission. France also had launched a unilateral military intervention in early 2013 to free northern towns from Islamist militant control, and pressed for both the African-led mission and the transition to a U.N.-conducted operation. MINUSMA was initially mandated to support Mali's transitional authorities in stabilizing "key population centers," support the extension of state authority throughout the country, and prepare for elections, in addition to protecting civilians and U.N. personnel, promoting human rights, and protecting humanitarian aid Unlike most U.N. peacekeeping operations in Africa, MINUSMA includes sizable Western contingents, including from Canada (134), Germany (381), the Netherlands (116), Norway (92),and Sweden (253).

The countries contributing the largest uniformed contingents (+1,000 each), however, are nearby (Burkina Faso, Chad, Senegal, Togo) or major global peacekeeping troop contributors (Bangladesh, Egypt).

MINUSMA is the world's deadliest current U.N. peacekeeping operation, with 126 personnel cumulatively killed in "malicious acts" Policymakers debated, in particular, whether U.N. personnel would be adequately protected and whether a U.N.

operation could or should be given a counterterrorism mandate. Ultimately, MINUSMA was not given an explicit mandate to conduct counterterrorism or counterinsurgency operations. France, meanwhile, has maintained troops in the country as a de facto parallel force to target terrorist cells, a mission for which the U.S. military provides direct logistical support.

The Mali mission is the only U.N. peacekeeping operations that authorizes troops to deter and counter terrorist groups that can harm its work or civilians. Last year, the U.N. Security Council said the mission should become "more proactive and robust" — many see that as encouraging more offensive operations.

The major problem is the U.N. missions lack the resources, doctrine and training for counterterrorism work. he United Nations now has a fleet of surveillance drones and first U.N. intelligence cell, with analysts spread across the country plus counter-IED specialists. UN forces now include large contingents from Germany, the Netherlands and Sweden, with soldiers experienced in fighting in Afghanistan.

Unfortunately the terrorists appear stronger than ever. French forces conduct its own counterterrorism mission in Mali and the United Nations shares information with the French if it is deemed useful for protecting the lives of troops.

With a current peace agreement between Mali parties supported by the UN Mali is slowly working its way back to a level of stability.

71. MINUSCA - U.N. Multidimensional Integrated Stabilization Mission in Central African Republic

MINUSCA: The ribbon has two United Nations blue stripes on the edges, followed by alternating dark blue, white, red, yellow and green stripes which are the colors of the CAR flag adopted in 1958.

Country/Location	Central African Republic
Dates	2014 to Present
Countries Participating	Military personnel: Austria, Albania, Bangladesh, Bolivia, Brazil, Benin, Burkina Faso, Croatia, Cambodia, Democratic Republic of the Congo, Denmark, Ecuador, Ethiopia, Egypt, France, Finland, Gabon, Gambia, Ghana, Italy, Ireland, Jordan, Kenya, Kyrgyzstan, Mongolia, Malawi, Mali, Norway, Nepal, Nigeria, Namibia, Poland, Pakistan, Paraguay, Portugal, Russian Federation, Rwanda, Sri Lanka, Serbia, Senegal, Spain, Togo, Tunisia, Uganda, United States, Uruguay, Yemen and Zambia.
	Police personnel: Benin, Burkina Faso, Burundi, Cameroon, Côte d'Ivoire, Egypt, Finland, France, Guinea, Jordan, Libya, Madagascar, Mali, Niger, Portugal, Rwanda, Senegal, Sweden, Togo, Turkey and Yemen.
Maximum Srength	1,650military personnel, 2,080 Police, Appropiate civilian component
Current Strength	14,708
Fatalities	97
Medal Number	71
CLASP(S)	None

MANDATE:: The Security Council established the U.N. Multidimensional Integrated Stabilization Mission in CAR (MINUSCA) in 2014 in response to a spiraling conflict and humanitarian crisis in the country. The crisis began in 2013 when a largely Muslim-led rebel coalition seized control of the central government; largely Christian- and animist-led militias emerged in response and brutally targeted Muslim civilians, resulting in a pattern of killings and large-scale displacement that U.N.investigators later termed "ethnic cleansing."

BACKGROUND: MINUSCA absorbed a preexisting African intervention force, as well as a U.N. political mission in CAR. Although CAR returned to elected civilian-led government in 2016, rebel groups continue to control most of the countryside. Armed factions have continued to kill and abuse civilians, often along sectarian and ethnic lines.

Despite nearly reaching its full authorized troop ceiling, MINUSCA continues to exhibit operational capacity shortfalls, which the Security Council has attributed to "undeclared national policy, lack of effective command and control, refusal to obey orders, failure to respond to attacks on civilians, and inadequate equipment."

Continued violence has fueled local frustrations with MINUSCA's perceived ineffectiveness—as has a sweeping sexual abuse scandal implicating multiple MINUSCA contingents, coupled with French units deployed under their national command. Hostility has also been driven by government officials who oppose a U.N. arms embargo on the country, as well as local leaders who seek to discredit international forces and destabilize the government.

Whether a peace accord signed in early 2019 will bring greater stability remains to be seen. MINUSCA is currently mandated to protect civilians, support the extension of state authority, assist the peace process, and protect humanitarian aid delivery, among other tasks. It also has an unusual mandate to pursue "urgent temporary measures ... to arrest and detain in order to maintain basic law and order and fight impunity," under certain conditions. The mission has employed this authority against several militia leaders, with mixed effects on local security.

The Trump Administration has maintained support to date, and in 2017 backed a troop ceiling increase of 900 military personnel.

UN Photo

72. MINUJUSTH - U.N. Multidimensional Integrated Stabilization Mission in Haiti

MINUJUSTH: The color combination for the ribbon consists of the royal blue and red of the Republic of Haiti to the left and right of a center stripe UN blue with two white lines denoting friendship between the two.

Country/Location	Haiti
Dates	2017 - 15 October 2019
Countries Participating	Senegal, Canada, Benin, Jordon, Rwanda, Niger, Mali, Napal ,Tunisia, Madagascar
Maximum Srength	295 Police, 325 Civilians
Current Strength	0
Fatalities	1
Medal Number	72
CLASP(S)	None

MANDATE: The mandate of the United Nations Mission for Justice Support in Haiti (MINUJUSTH) is set out in the Security Council Resolution 2350 (2017), which was adopted on 13 April 2017. It provided for the establishment of a peacekeeping mission in Haiti that would begin operations upon completion of the mandate of the United Nations Stabilization Mission in Haiti (MINUSTAH). The Mission will be composed of 351 civilian staff, up to seven Formed Police Units (FPUs) (comprised of 980 FPU personnel) and 295 Individual Police Officers (IPOs), for an initial period of six months from 16 October 2017 until 15 April 2018.

BACKGROUND: MINUJUSTH assisted the Government of Haiti to further develop the Haitian National Police (HNP); to strengthen Haiti's rule of law institutions, including the justice and prisons; and to promote and protect human rights - all with a view to improving the everyday lives of the Haitian people.

The United Nations long-standing peacekeeping presence in Haiti closed its doors in October 2019 amid mounting political and security challenges, which risk eroding strides facilitated by a generation of blue helmets, said the Organization's senior peace operations official in a briefing to the Security Council.

"The current context is not an ideal way to end 15 years of peacekeeping," said Jean-Pierre LaCroix, Under-Secretary-General for Peace Operations. Presenting the Secretary-General's final report on the United Nations Mission for Justice Support in Haiti (MINUJUSTH) — he warned the 15-member Council that a political stalemate in Haiti is leading to deteriorating security, violent protests and disruptions in humanitarian support. Haitians remain largely dissatisfied with their leaders and at least 30 people were reported killed during protests between 15 September and 9 October.

Noting that President Jovenel Moïse's Government has not yet received confirmation in the Parliament, he warned that legislative elections cannot take place amid the stalemate and the stage is now set for an institutional vacuum. Calling on all parties to reject violence, he said the many strides achieved in the past 15 years — especially in reducing community violence, strengthening human rights and fostering accountability for victims — should not mask Haiti's significant ongoing challenges. Emphasizing that the closure of MINUJUSTH does not represent the Organization's departure, he said the shift to the United Nations Integrated Office in Haiti (BINUH) presents an opportunity to recenter the Organization's priorities.

73. UNHQ UNITED NATIONS HEADQUARTERS MEDAL

UNHQ: Member countries provide, military staff officers to serve in staff positions in the New York United Nations Headquarters to assist with the planning and implementation of new peacekeeping missions. These officers may be awarded the United Nations Headquarters Service Medal after 90 days of service.

BACKGROUND: From the earliest days of United Nations involvement in the deployment, supply and support of peace-keeping missions in the field, it was quite obvious that a cadre of resident staff officers, fully-trained in planning of a military nature, would be required at United Nations Headquarters. For this reason, experienced military and naval personnel, drawn from the armed forces of the member nations, may be temporarily assigned to the United Nations Headquarters in New York to perform the vital tasks of planning and implementation of new missions. To reward such activities, the United Nations Headquarters Medal, having the standard UN planchet with a solid UN blue ribbon may be awarded after 90 days of service.

MEDAL NO.: 73   **CLASP(S):** None

UN Photo

74. UNSSM UNITED NATIONS SPECIAL SERVICES MEDAL

UNSSM: Established in June 1995 this medal recognizes military personnel and civilian police serving the United Nations in capacities other than established peacekeeping missions and United Nations Headquarters. The colour combination consists of a large blue stripe framed between two white stripes. In order to identify the theater in which the personnel will have earned the medal, a bar is added with the name of the country or the United Nations organization (UNHCR, UNSCOM, etc)ribbon bar.

BACKGROUND: Established in 1994 by the Secretary-General of the United Nations, the United Nations Medal for Special Service is awarded to military and civilian police personnel serving the United Nations in capacities other than established peace-keeping missions or those permanently assigned to United Nations Headquarters (see medal 73). The Medal for Special Service may be awarded to eligible personnel serving for a minimum of ninety (90) consecutive days under the control of the United Nations in operations or offices for which no other United Nations award is authorized. Posthumous awards may be granted to personnel otherwise eligible for the medal who die while serving under the United Nations before completing the required 90 consecutive days of service.

MEDAL NO: 74

CLASP(S): Clasps engraved with the name of the country or the United Nations organization (e.g., UNHCR, UNSCOM, MINUGUA, etc.) may be added to the medal suspension ribbon and ribbon bar.

The UN envoy to Somalia, James Swan, pins a medal on a UN military advisor during a medal award ceremony at the UN compound in Mogadishu. At least 13 officers were awarded UN special service medals in recognition of their contribution to ongoing peace efforts in Somalia. UN Photo / Omar Abdisalan

Other Peace Keeping Operations

International Commission for Supervision and Control (ICSC)

Dates: 1954 to 1965

Location: Indochina (Republic of Vietnam)

Countries Participating: Canada, India, Poland

Notes: The commission was established by the Geneva peace agreements of 1954 to supervise the partition of Indochina after the departure of the French. The medal was awarded to personnel assigned to the commission for a 90 day tour of duty after August 7, 1954. The medal has the flags of Canada and Poland with the Indian symbol of three lions of the Asoka Pillar, with a flying dove in the center and the inscription around the sides INTERNATIONAL COMMISSION FOR SUPERVISION AND CONTROL, and below PEACE. The back of the medal has a map of Indochina , with the names of the countries in native script. The green in the ribbon represents India, the red Canada and Poland. Canadian regulation (CFAO 18-8) required the recipient's rank and name be engraved around the edge of the medal. The blacken bronze medal was reportedly struck in Bangalore, India with a gilt version done in Canada for 1403 Canadians.

Background: There are three varieties of this first version, respectively with a raised small maple leaf between the tips at the top of the back, with an incused maple leaf, and with no maple leaf. The first two varieties were clearly manufactured just for the Canadian contingent with the Commission.

Second Version

International Commission of Control and Supervision (ICCS)

Second Version

Dates: 1973 to 1975

Location: Indochina (Republic of Vietnam)

Countries Participating: Canada, Hungary, Indonesia, Poland

Notes: The second Indochina peace commission was established by the Paris peace agreements of 1973 to investigate violations of the accords following the cessation of hostilities. The medal was awarded to personnel assigned to the commission for a 90 day tour of duty in Vietnam. Two distinct versions were issued with identical medals but having different ribbons. The first (left medal) was awarded to most of the personnel involved, but the second design (right medal) was apparently awarded only to 355 Canadian participants. There were 3 versions of the first medal, one with a raised maple leaf, one with an incused maple leaf, and one with no maple leaf. The medal has symbols for the four participating countries, the Canadian maple leaf, Hungarian Coat of Arms, Indonesian Garuda, and Polish Eagle. The inscription INTERNATIONAL COMMISSION OF CONTROL AND SUPERVISION runs around the outside. The back reads; SERVICE VIETNAM 27-1, 1973 bracketed by two sprays of laurel leaves.

Other Peace Keeping Operations

Organization of American States (O.A.S.)

Dates: 1965 to 1966

Location: Dominican Republic

Countries Participating: Brazil, Costa Rica, El Salvador, Honduras, Nicaragua, Paraguay, United States

    Notes: The above-mentioned nations formed the Inter-American Peace Force (IAPF) during the Dominican Republic internal power struggle which occurred in 1965. At its height, the IAPF was composed of approximately 13,000 troops from the United States and 1,700 personnel from the other six Latin-American countries. To commemorate this operation, the U.S. Army Institute of Heraldry designed a medal to be awarded to American personnel as well as to the other foreign nationals involved. However, owing to other political considerations, the medal was never issued and United States participants were awarded the existing Armed Forces Expeditionary Medal instead.

Multinational Force and Observers (MFO)

Dates: 1982 to Present

Location: Sinai Desert (Egypt, formerly occupied by Israel)

Countries Participating: Australia, Canada, Columbia, Fiji, France, Italy, Netherlands, New Zealand, United Kingdom, United States, Uruguay

    Notes: Established by the Camp David Accords and the peace treaty of 1979 between Egypt and Israel to monitor the withdrawal of Israeli forces from the Sinai Desert. Medal is awarded for six (6) months service in the Sinai Peninsula (Sinai Desert). First awarded to individuals who served 90 days, with the time increased to 170 days minimum after 15 March 1985. The reverse of the medal has a raised inscription UNITED IN SERVICE FOR PEACE set in five straight lines. The only difference between the military and civilian versions is the ribbon. The military ribbon consists of three equal parts orange-white-orange, separated by 1/8 inch wide stripes of olive green. The Civilian version consists of three equal parts of olive green-white-olive green with 3/16 inch wide orange edges. All other comments and requirements are identical.

International Conference on the Former Yugoslavia (ICFY)

Dates: 1993 to 1996

Location: Former Yugoslavia

Countries Participating: Belgium, Canada, Czech Republic, Denmark, Finland, France, Germany, Greece, Ireland, Italy, Netherlands, Norway, Portugal, Russian Federation, Spain, Sweden, United Kingdom, United States

Notes: In 1992, the countries of the European Community formed the above conference group to provide a forum for negotiation and discussion of regional problems after the breakup of the Former Yugoslavia. The medal was created by the European Community and awarded after 90 days of service. Although the United Nations participated officially in the planning and execution of the Conference, it did not sanction nor authorize the medal.

The NATO Meritorious Service Medal

The NATO Meritorious Service Medal

The NATO **Meritorious Service Medal** was established in 2003 for military and civilian personnel commended for providing exceptional or remarkable service to NATO. The Medal is the personal Award of The Secretary General of NATO, who signs each citation. Generally fewer than 50 medals are awarded each year and it is the only significant award for individual effort on the NATO staff. It can be awarded to both Military and Civilian staff. The criteria for the award reflects: the performance of acts of courage in difficult or dangerous circumstances; showing exceptional leadership or personal example; making an outstanding individual contribution to a NATO sponsored program or activity; or enduring particular hardship or deprivation in the interest of NATO.

The ribbon and medal fabric is NATO Blue with white edges, with silver and gold threads centered on the white. The medal disc is of silver color, occasional you will see copies being sold with the regular brass medallion. The NATO Meritorious Service Medal is now authorized for wear on U.S. Military uniforms.

North Atlantic Treaty Organization Medals

Awarded to NATO military personnel for service under the NATO command and in direct support of NATO operations. Recipients may qualify for such NATO operations as:

(1) Former Yugoslavia: 30 days service inside or 90 days outside the former Republic of Yugoslavia after July 1, 1992 to a date to be determined.

(2) Kosovo: 30 continuous/accumulated days in or around the former Yugoslavian province of Kosovo from October 13, 1998 to a date to be determined.

Multiple rotations or tours in either operational area will only qualify for a single award of that medal.

The NATO Medal, like the United Nations Medal, has a common planchet/pendant but comes with unique ribbons for each operation. As in the case of the United Nations, U.S. Service personnel who qualify for both NATO Medals will wear the first medal/ribbon awarded and a bronze service star on the ribbon bar and suspension ribbon to denote the second award. As before however, the two medal clasps which may accompany the medal. i.e., "FORMER YUGOSLAVIA and KOSOVO" may not be worn on the U.S. military uniform.

The medal is a bronze disk featuring the NATO symbol in the center surrounded by olive branches around the periphery. The reverse contains the inscription, "NORTH ATLANTIC TREATY ORGANIZATION" in English around the top edge and the same wording in French along the lower edge. A horizontal olive branch separates the central area into two areas. Atop this, set in three lines, is the inscription, "IN SERVICE OF PEACE AND FREEDOM" in English. The same text in French on four lines is inscribed in the lower half.

In November, 2002, the NATO Military Committee issued a new NATO Medal Policy in which two classes of service awards will now be issued, namely "Article 5" and "Non-Article 5". The reference is to Article 5 of the original NATO Charter Treaty in which the member nations agreed that an armed attack against any one of them in Europe or North America shall be considered an attack against them all and if such an armed attack occurs, each of them will take such action, including the use of armed force, to restore and maintain the security of the North Atlantic area. Non-Article 5 operations are those conducted as a peace support or crisis operation authorized by the North Atlantic Council.

To date, two Article 5 Medals have been issued by NATO, the first being for Operation "Eagle Assist". Following the 9-11 attacks, NATO Early Warning aircraft were deployed from October 12, 2001 to May 16, 2002, to monitor the airspace over the United States to protect against further airborne attack by terrorists.

The second award, is awarded to personnel who took part in Operation "Active Endeavor", the deployment of a NATO Standing Naval Force to patrol the Eastern Mediterranean against hostile forces. That effort began on October 26, 2001 and will be terminated at a date

NATO Medal

Service: All Services
Instituted: 1992
Criteria: 30 days service in or 90 days outside the former Republic of Yugoslavia and the Adriatic Sea under NATO command in direct support of NATO operations.
Devices:

Notes: *Above date denotes when award was authorized for wear by U.S. military personnel. "Former Yugoslavia" and "Kosovo" Bars not authorized for wear by U.S. Military personnel.*

Article 5 NATO Medal

Service: All Services
Instituted: 2002
Criteria: 30 days service as part of Operation "Eagle Assist" (Medal 1) or Operation Active Endeavor (Medal 2).
Devices:

Notes: *As per a memorandum issued by the Deputy Secretary of Defense dated 2 March 2006, the above medals are now authorized for wear on the uniform by U.S. military personnel.*

Non-Article 5 NATO Medal and ISAF Medal

Service: All Services
Instituted: 2002
Criteria: 30 days service as part of NATO operations in the Balkans (Medal 3) of Afghanistan (Medal 4).
Devices:

Notes: *As per a memorandum issued by the Deputy Secretary of Defense dated 2 March 2006, the above medals are now authorized for wear on the uniform by U.S. military personnel.*

to be announced in the future. In addition, two Non-Article 5 NATO have been authorized for U.S. military personnel. The qualification period for the NATO Balkans Medal is thirty days of continuous or accumulated service from January 1, 2003 to a date to be determined. The NATO medals for Afghanistan and Iraq are also awarded for 30 days of service in country.

United Nations Service Medal (Korea)

Service: All Services
Instituted: 1951
Criteria: Service on behalf of the United Nations in Korea between 27 June 1950 and 27 July 1954.
Devices: None

Notes: *Above date denotes when award was authorized for wear by U.S. military personnel.*

Originally, U.S. military personnel serving with United Nations Missions were permitted to wear only two UN medals, the United Nations Korean Service Medal and the United Nations Medal *(shown to the right)*. However, changes in Department of Defense policy in 1996 authorized the wear of the ribbons of 11 missions on the U.S. military uniform.

In 2011 sixteen more missions were added to the list, which, along with the United Nations Special Service Medal, brought the total to 28. However, only one ribbon (or medal) may be worn on the U.S. military uniform and awards for any subsequent missions are denoted by the three-sixteenth inch bronze stars.

United Nations Medal

Service: All Services
Instituted: 1964
Criteria: 6 months service with any authorized UN mission.
Devices:

Notes: *Medal worn with appropriate mission ribbon. (See below for complete list).*

UNTSO United Nations Truce Supervision Organization Country/Location: **Israel, Egypt** Dates: **1948 - Present**	**UNMOGIP** United Nations Military Observer Group in India/Pakistan Country/Location: **India, Pakistan** Dates: **1949 - Present**	**UNOGIL** United Nations Observer Group in Lebanon Country/Location: **Lebanon** Dates: **1958**

UNSF/UNTEA United Nations Security Force in West Guinea (West Irian) Country/Location: **West New Guinea (West Irian)** Dates: **1962 - 1963**	**UNIKOM** United Nations Iraq/Kuwait Observation Mission Country/Location: **Iraq/Kuwait** Dates: **1991 - 2003**	**MINURSO** United Nations Mission for the Referendum in Western Sahara Country/Location: **Morocco** Dates: **1991 to Present**

UNAMIC United Nations Advance Mission in Cambodia Country/Location: **Cambodia** Dates: **1991 -1992**	**UNPROFOR** United Nations Protection Force Country/Location: **Former Yoguslavia, (Bosnia, Herzegovina, Croatia, Serbia, Montenegro, Macedonia)** Dates: **1992 - 1995**	**UNTAC** United Nations Transitional Authority in Cambodia Country/Location: **Cambodia** Dates: **1992 - 1993**

ONUMOZ
United Nations Operation in Mozanbique
Country/Location: **Mozanbique**
Dates: **1992 - 1994**

UNOSOM II
United Nations Operation in Somalia II
Country/Location: **Somalia**
Dates: **1993 - 1995**

UNOMIG
United Nations Observer
Mission in Georgia
Country/Location: **Georgia (Russia)**
Dates:**1993 - 2009**

UNMIH
United Nations Mission in Haiti
Country/Location: **Haiti**
Dates: **1993 - 1996**

UNPREDEP
United Nations Prevention
Deployment Force
Country/Location: **Former
Yugoslavia; Republic of Macedonia**
Dates: **1995 - 1999**

UNTAES
United Nations Transitional Administration
for Eastern Slavonia, Baranja
and Western Sirmium
Country/Location: **Croatia**
Dates: 1996 - **1998**

UNSMIH
United Nations Support
Mission in Haiti
Country/Location: **Haiti**
Dates: **1996 - 1997**

MINUGUA
United Nations Verification
Mission in Guatemala
Country/Location: **Guatemala**
Dates: **1997-1997**

UNMIK
United Nations Interim
Administration Mission in Kosovo
Country/Location: **Kosovo**
Dates: **1999 - Present**

UNTAET
United Nations Transitional
Administration in East Timor
Country/Location: **Timor (New Guinea)**
Dates: **1999 - 2002**

MONUC
United Nations Organization Mission in
the Democratic Republic of the Congo
Country/Location: **Congo**
Dates: **1999 - 2010**

UNMEE
United Nations Mission to Ethiopia
and Eritrea
Country/Location: **Ethiopia, Eritrea**
Dates: **2000 - 2008**

UNMISET
United Nations Mission of
Support in East Timor
Country/Location: **Timor (New Guinea)**
Dates: **2000 - 2005**

UNMIL
United Nations Mission in Liberia
Country/Location: **Liberia
(West Africa)**
Dates: **2003 - 2018**

MINUSTAH
United Nations Stabilization
Mission in Haiti
Country/Location: **Haiti**
Dates: **2004 - 2017**

UNAMID
United Nations / African Union Hybrid
Operation in Darfur
Country/Location: **Darfur (East Africa)**
Dates: **2007 - 2020**

MINURCAT
United Nations Mission in the Central
African Republic and Chad
Country/Location: **Central African
Republic, Chad (Central Africa)**
Dates: **2007 - 2010**

MONUSCO
United Nations Organization
Stabilization Mission in the Democratic
Republic of the Congo
Country/Location: **Congo**
Dates: **2010 - Present**

United Nations Special Service Medal UNSSM

Background: Established in 1994 by the Secretary General of the United Nations, the UNSSM is awarded to military and civilian personnel service in capacities other than established peace-keeping missions or those permanently assigned to UN Headquarters. The UNSSM may be awarded to eligible personnel service for a minimum of ninety (90) consecutive days under the control of the UN in operations or offices for which no other United Nations award is authorized. Posthumous awards may be granted to personnel otherwise eligible for the medal who died while serving under the United Nations before completing the required 90 days of service.
Clasps: Clasps engraved with the name of the country or United Nations organization (e.g.: UNHCR, UNSCOM, UNAMI, etc.) may be added to the medal suspension ribbon and ribbon bar.

BIBLIOGRAPHY

Blue Helmets, The: A review of United Nations Peacekeeping Forces, third edition, 1996, United Nations Press

Borts, L.H.- United Nations Medals and Missions, 1997, Medals of America Press

Brown, J. D., India, Life World Library, 1967, time – Life Books

Dept. of Defense Manual DOD 1348.33M- Manual of Military Decorations & Awards, 1996

Dorling, H.T. - Ribbons and Medals, 1983

Foster, Frank. Complete Guide to United States Army Medals, Badges and Insignia, 2004.

Foster, Frank. Military Medals of America, 2019.

Foster, Frank. United States Army Medals, Badges and Insignia, 2011.

Foster, Frank and Sylvester, John. The Decorations and Medals of the Republic of Vietnam and Her Allies, 1950-1975, 1995. Medals of America Press

Gardam, Col. John, The Canadian peacekeeper, 1992, Gen. Store Publishing House, Inc.

Gleim, A. F. And McDowell, C. P. – United Nations Korean Service Medal, 1990, Fox Press Inc

Inter-American Defense Board- Norms for Protocol, Symbols, Insignia and Gifts, 1984

Joslin, E. C., Litherland, A. R. And Simpkin, B. T. – British Battles and Medals, 1988, Spink and Son limited London

Kerrigan, E.- American Medals and Decorations, 1990

Kerrigan, E.- American War Medals and Decorations, 1971

McLaughlin, Donal – Origin of the Emblem and Other Recollections of the San Francisco Conference, 1945, United Nations archives

Oliver, Ray. "What's In A Name?," 1983.

Pitta, John and McCouaig, Simon – UN Forces, 1948 to 1994, Elite series, 1994, Osprey publishing, Limited

Pownall, Henry – Korean Campaign Medals, 1954, Gothic Press Limited

Rosignoli, Guido. Badges and Insignia of World War II, 1980

Rosignoli, G. - The Illustrated Encyclopedia of Military Insignia of the 20th Century

Sargent, J. L., Turkish United Nations Korean Medal, The Medal Collector, OMSA journal, November 1984

Sylvester, J., Colors and Politics: Ribbons of the United Nations Medals for Cambodia, OMSA Journal, April 1996 U.S.

United Nations Peacekeeping, (pamphlet), August., 1993, United Nations Department of Public Information

U.S.Army Regulation 670-1- Wear and Appearance of Army Uniforms and Insignia, May, 2000

U.S. Army Regulation 600-8-22- Military Awards, 1995

U.S. Army Regulation 672-5 - Military Awards, 1990.

Vietnam Council on Foreign Relations- Awards & Decorations of Vietnam, 1972

INDEX

Press

Other Great Medals and Insignia Books All Available at
WWW.MOAPress.com
or on Amazon

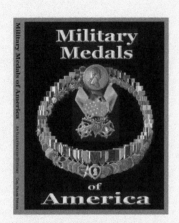

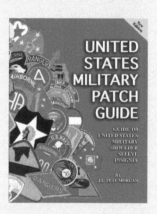

America's Best Medal and Ribbon Wear Guides All Available
at WWW.MOAPress.com
or on Amazon